HUNDREDFOLD

HUNDREDFOLD

A GUIDE TO PARISH VOCATION MINISTRY

RHONDA GRUENEWALD

VIANNEY VOCATIONS

Vianney Vocations LLC
Valdosta, GA 31601
www.vianneyvocations.com

Printed in the United States of America
First Edition

ISBN: 978-0-9896212-3-6

LCCN: 2015940306

Nihil obstat: Rev. Douglas K. Clark, STL
Imprimatur: Most Rev. Gregory J. Hartmayer, OFM Conv., D.D., Diocese of Savannah

Cover photo © Life Teen. Cover design by Sam Alzheimer

This book is dedicated to the men and women who have said "Yes" to Christ. They serve as an inspiration for each of us to live with an openness to what God wants for our lives.

CONTENTS

PART II

FOREWORD

It is no secret that many priest-pastors these days do not actively promote priestly and religious vocations in their parishes. I can certainly speak to this, since I am a priest-pastor. It is not that these priests do not desire more vocations in the Church. It is simply that these priests are *tired*. When someone mentions that the parish really should be doing much more to keep priesthood and religious life front and center, the priest usually sighs and says, "Yes, I know." The fact is that because we have fewer priests, the priests we do have are busier than ever.

Yet this is the age of the laity! In the spirit of *Christifidelis Laici*, the 1988 document of St. John Paul II, commemorating 20 years since the Second Vatican Council, the present Church calls all people in every vocation to step up and do what needs to be done to bring Jesus Christ to the world. Lay people are doing amazing work in the Catholic Church in catechesis and evangelization, often things that no priest or religious sister would be able to do. Even in the promotion of vocations, lay people can step up to establish and maintain that vital culture of vocations in their local parishes which will unfailingly grow our future priests and religious.

Rhonda Gruenewald has done just that. Twelve years after her conversion to the Catholic Faith, Rhonda recognized the call of God to establish a vocation ministry in her own parish. Through this process, she learned many valuable lessons and persevered through numerous obstacles. In the end, the work was very successful and her parish continues to be a flagship of what a dedicated parish vocation ministry should be! God orchestrated all of this, I believe, not only to foster vocations at St. Cecilia parish in Houston, but also to equip her to write this book.

Hundredfold is a how-to manual with a wealth of wonderful ideas for creating a culture of vocations. Rhonda explains how to establish and support a parish vocation ministry in a way that is not frightening or intimidating. Just reading the book makes a person excited; you will probably find yourself thinking, "We can do this!" The book will be a great blessing to bishops, vocation directors, and parish priests in mobilizing parish vocation ministries.

St. Ignatius Loyola wrote: "Work as if it all depends on you. Pray as if it all depends on God." Yes, the ministry of vocations will not be successful without both work and prayer.

Blessed Hanibal di Francia wrote: "Jesus wanted to teach us that vocations in the Church do not come by chance, neither by themselves, nor can we make them out of human efforts only. They come to us from the mercy of God. If we do not pray to obtain them, they will not be given us."

Hundredfold recognizes these truths and builds upon them. As a priest-pastor, and a former vocation director and seminary vice-rector, I have initiated several efforts in my parish to promote vocations. But after reading this book, I am very confident that much more will be done in the coming years through parish vocation committees!

The greatest work in the Kingdom of God is not done at the Vatican in Rome or in the office of the local bishop, as important as they are. The greatest work in the Church is done in the local parish, initiated by the local people themselves. Their work, in turn, feeds into the work of the vocation directors for dioceses and religious orders. All of it is done to raise up vocations, but it starts locally.

This is the age of the laity. The Holy Spirit is moving dedicated men and women to help create a culture of vocations in the parish, a local greenhouse which will plant, nurture and produce holy priests and religious for the service of God's people. Give this book to your parish priest. That way, when someone comes up to him and says, "Father, the parish really should be doing much more to keep priesthood and religious life front and center," the priest will smile and give him a copy of *Hundredfold*. And he will say, "I will support you in this great work for the Church. Thank you for responding to God's call."

Fr. Brett Brannen
Savannah, May 2015

Author of *To Save a Thousand Souls: A Guide for Discerning a Vocation to Diocesan Priesthood*
and *A Priest in the Family: A Guide for Parents Whose Sons are Considering Priesthood*

ACKNOWLEDGMENTS

I first give thanks to God who has made this amazing journey possible. You placed this love of vocations deep within me, and I am forever grateful. All honor and glory are yours forever!

A special thank you to our intercessors. To our Blessed Mother, who covered our Vocation Ministry with her mantle of love, we continue to consecrate our ministry to Jesus through you, as your first "yes!" is an example to us all. St. Alphonsus Liguori, patron saint of vocations, whose intercession we seek for each activity, you have never failed to come to our aid!

I thank Father Victor Perez, who under the direction of Father John Cahoon, was asked to revive the Parish Vocation Committee at Saint Cecilia Catholic Church in 2011. Working with him for two years was a turning point for me. While volunteering in the parish was a joy already, vocations became an integral part of my everyday life. His example of living life for Christ in all ways encourages me to do the same in every way I can.

A special thanks to Margo Geddie, 2010-14 Governor of the District 10 Serra Clubs of Houston, Larry Massey, 2014-16 Governor, and the Serra Governor's Council for enthusiastically embracing me and our ministry. This book would simply not be a reality without their help and support.

Thank you to all the friends and family who have been supportive in the process of writing this manuscript. Thank you especially to those of you who read the early drafts and offered your thoughts and prayers. Special thanks to Father Dat Hoang, Sister Anita Brenek, Deacon Frank Davis, Katie Hartfiel, Kelly Wimberly, Susan and Larry Massey, Judy Cozzens, Mark Bonkiewicz, Michelle Migone, and Taylor Morgan.

This work would not have been possible without the support of my family. I thank David, my husband and champion, and my children Abby and Gabriel who encouraged my passion for vocations and sacrificed much for me to do this work. I also thank my mother, Kathy Fowler, for giving me the gift of words and encouraging me at each step of this process with love and kindness.

Finally, while I have the privilege of writing this book, it is the men and women of the Vocation Ministry and those who came before us at St. Cecilia Catholic Church who are the true heroes. They have risen to every occasion, working on behalf of vocations in any way asked. They have put forth the ideas and the efforts to affirm, promote, and, most importantly, pray for vocations. May God bless them and all who volunteer so freely to build up his kingdom here on Earth!

Rhonda Gruenewald
Houston, May 2015

INTRODUCTION

"Some seed fell on rich soil and produced fruit yielding thirty, sixty, and a hundredfold." ~Mark 4:8

The goal of this book is to provide inspiration to anyone starting or reviving a Vocation Ministry in his or her parish. It is written for the ordinary Catholic who wishes to get involved in promoting vocations, either by starting a brand-new committee or reinvigorating a long-standing committee with fresh ideas that attract new workers to the Lord's vineyard.

Why is this ministry needed? Over the past fifty years, the Catholic Church in the United States has experienced a tremendous decline in vocations to priesthood and religious life. Nearly 3,500 parishes in the United States do not have a resident pastor, which means that twenty percent of parishes do not have a priest to call their own![1] Similarly, as is widely known, the number of religious sisters has declined dramatically, to about a quarter of their number in the 1960s.[2]

Despite such figures, there is reason for hope. Some dioceses have bumper crops of fresh-faced, enthusiastic seminarians. Some parishes seem to produce new vocations every year. A few religious orders are bursting at the seams. To offer one popular example, the Nashville Dominicans (also known as The Dominican Sisters of St. Cecilia) have grown by 76 percent since 2000. Today, the community numbers over three hundred sisters.

---

1 www.cara.georgetown.edu/CARAServices/requestedchurchstats.html

2 www.cara.georgetown.edu/CARAServices/WomenReligious.pdf

Because of these success stories we can be certain that young people, even in our secular society, are still responding to the call to follow Jesus in a radical way. What is needed is for those who love the Church to work tirelessly to *create the environment* in which more young people can hear God's call. This book offers tried-and-true ways to do that. It is meant to be a practical guide for those working in a typical parish setting, large or small, urban or rural. Its aim is to help any parish to become one of the "vocation success stories."

Where to begin? This book moves from the theoretical (Part I) to the practical (Part II). Before a Vocation Ministry leaps into action, it's important to lay the groundwork. Chapter 1 clarifies the goals of the ministry. Chapter 2 provides experience-based guidance on administering a Vocation Ministry. Chapter 3 offers critical insight on the four phases of starting a Vocation Ministry so that eager members can pace themselves, working on simple projects first, like a Holy Hour for Vocations, before tackling complex initiatives like an event for seminarians.

Many readers will be more interested in Part II, which is dedicated to the activities themselves. The activities are listed in progressive order of complexity with regard to content, execution, and resources. Step-by-step instructions lay out the process of executing each activity, and a notes section provides additional background information and recommendations.

Each activity in Chapters 4-7 suggests resources to carry out that activity. Most resources referenced can be found at www.vocationministry. com, including downloads, examples, and videos that augment the information in this book.

Imagine the menu at your favorite restaurant where you go to celebrate special occasions. When you go to this restaurant, you cannot eat every dish on the menu, but the three items you select—appetizer, entrée, and dessert—satisfy you immensely. The next year when you come back, you select more items. These activity chapters are like that menu. Each ministry will select different activities for their parish. They will keep coming back for old favorites like Adoration for Vocations each year while also trying new items like a Lenten Fish Fry for Vocations. Each ministry can walk away feeling satisfied with its choices.

A word about the terminology used in the book. As can be expected, approaches differ among parishes, dioceses, and regions. For our purposes here, the term "ministry director" refers to the lay person in charge of the Vocation Ministry (or "vocation committee" as it is sometimes called). A member of the ministry who oversees a specific project is called a "coordinator." The term "ministry head" refers to the priest who is ultimately the overseer of the group.

Promoting vocations at the parish level is exciting, meaningful, essential work. Before undertaking any new task or activity, St. Aloysius Gonzaga asked the question, "What will it be worth for Eternity?" Each priest, religious, and married person comes into contact with hundreds or even thousands of people over the course of their lives. By praying for, bringing awareness to, and affirming these vocations, many other souls will be touched. The ripple effect from the work of a single Vocation Ministry could be more like a tsunami.

Pope Francis acknowledged this during an address to a large crowd during the 51st World Day of Prayer for Vocations. He said, "No vocation is born of itself or lives for itself. A vocation flows from the heart of God and blossoms in the good soil of faithful people, in the experience of fraternal love."[3]

---

3 Pope Francis: "Listen and Follow Jesus" for Day of Prayer for Vocations

PART
I

CHAPTER ONE

THE MISSION

If a family visited your parish on any given Sunday, would they know that your parish is serious about promoting vocations? What if the same family showed up on World Day of Prayer for Vocations? Would the parents notice that the parish was observing a special day? Would their children feel inspired to consider priesthood or religious life?

If you answered no to any of these questions, you are not alone. Most of the 17,400 Catholic parishes in the United States simply do not place a priority on fostering vocations. Sure, many parishes hang the annual seminarian poster in the church. Some pastors pray for vocations during Mass. Undoubtedly catechists mention Holy Orders while reviewing the seven sacraments. But more often than not, these actions are unorganized, not part of a deliberate parish-wide effort to help young people consider God's call for their lives. This needs to change. Every parish needs a dedicated group or committee—which in this book is called a "Vocation Ministry"—tasked with the important work of promoting vocations.

The overall mission of any Catholic parish is to help its members fulfill their primary vocation: to grow in holiness. Within this broad context, a Vocation Ministry has a narrower task: to help parishioners (especially youth) discern God's will for their specific vocations.

While working toward this goal, instead of counting how many priests and sisters a parish produces, it's better to focus on creating the environment where young people can hear and answer God's call. Then let the Holy Spirit do the rest. If the ministry focuses on prayer, education, and encouragement, the mission will be accomplished. Over time, vocations will increase, including more seminarians, more men and women in religious orders, and more holy, faithful marriages.

Why in the Parish?

Every pope for at least the last century has pointed out that vocations begin in the family. This is easy to accept. Everyone can observe that even small children "catch" the faith from the teaching and example of their parents. When the family's faith is especially strong, vocations flourish. One need only reference the vocation stories of thousands of clergy (including bishops and popes), who credit their devout mothers with their priestly vocations. Once we recognize that families are the seedbeds of vocations, the question becomes: where do the families themselves receive their formation?

The answer is easy: families are formed in *parishes*. That is simply the way that the Church is structured. Of course, parents probably receive formation from other sources such as Catholic media, but their regular, ongoing, weekly encounter with the Church and the sacraments happens in ordinary parishes.

This is why parish-based Vocation Ministry is so critical. There's simply no replacing it. Diocesan Vocation Offices organize terrific events for young men and women. Various religious orders offer inspiring weekend retreats. But as valuable as these are, they simply can't replace on-the-ground, consistent formation in parishes. Inspiring children and teens has to happen where they are. For every diocesan-level youth rally, there are thirty ordinary youth ministry meetings in the parish hall. This humble setting is where youth need to be inspired to become open to God's call—whether to marriage, priesthood, or religious life.

Studies also show that a large number of young men and women are discouraged from considering a vocation to priesthood or religious life. The Vocation Ministry needs to build up a culture of vocations at the parish level so that friends and family members feel comfortable and happy to affirm those young men and women who are discerning this call.

Research supports the idea that parish-based Vocation Ministry is crucial. The following graph shows that the majority of young men and almost as many young women consider a religious vocation between 13

WHEN IN YOUR LIFE DID YOU FIRST CONSIDER A RELIGIOUS VOCATION?

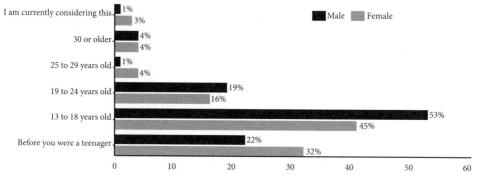

http://cara.georgetown.edu/Publications/NurturingVocations.pdf

and 18 years of age. At the risk of sounding obvious, these are the ages when children live in their parents' home, ride in the family minivan to Mass, and participate in various parish catechesis programs. Like their parents, these teens may encounter inspiration outside the parish environment, but by and large, the parish is the "home base" for their faith.

Perhaps surprisingly, a very large number of these Catholic youth are open to the idea of priesthood and religious life. Another survey of never-married Catholics ages 14 and older revealed that between 4-5% considered priesthood or religious life "a little seriously." This translates to 1.4 million young men and 1.3 million young women. The potential here is great!

The same survey found that 2-3% of the respondents considered a priestly or religious vocation "very seriously," which translates to 353,000 young men and 255,000 young women who are thinking about a possible future as a priest, sister or brother. However, one needs only look at seminary enrollment (about 4,000) to see that, for whatever reason, this serious interest has not materialized beyond an idea.

Studies like these should provoke new thinking about how to promote vocations. The implication is that teens in parishes, many of whom are at least open to the idea of a vocation, need better education, inspiration, and support so that their vocations can mature. This takes "planting seeds" through education and invitation. It requires creating opportunities for the Holy Spirit to reach the hearts of young discerners. It also takes the support of adults dedicated to prayer and encouragement.

When promoting vocations, it's important to be aware of the realities within different Catholic ethnic groups, most notably the Hispanic community. As of 2014, 35% of the total U.S. population was Hispanic, but less than 5% of priests ordained that same year were Hispanic. This has led the U.S. bishops to make fostering priestly vocations among Hispanics a strategic priority. Nearly two-thirds of young Hispanic Catholics are born in the United States, so Vocation Ministries need to increase awareness and opportunities for those youth to open their hearts in a real way to God's call.[4]

Thankfully, there is much hope! But to reap the potential harvest, more parishes need a dedicated Vocation Ministry that focuses on helping youth hear and respond to Jesus' call.

The Ideal Vocation-minded Parish

Fast-forward a few years from now. Imagine that your parish has an established Vocation Ministry with enthusiastic and committed members who meet regularly. Now envision a family visiting for Mass, perhaps on Priesthood Sunday, which is celebrated on the last Sunday in October. Here are a few things they might experience:

- A banner announcing a special day to honor the parish priests
- Book rack materials in the church narthex that explain priesthood to youth
- An announcement at Mass acknowledging the celebration of Priesthood Sunday
- A bulletin blurb that specifically recognizes the priests, accompanied by a short biography of their life and priestly service
- Ushers offering prayer cards to take home and pray for the parish priests or priests in general

---

4 http://usccb.org/beliefs-and-teachings/vocations/priesthood/priestly-life-and-ministry/
upload/McKnight-NOCERCC-11Feb2015.pdf

- A prayer drive activity, where parishioners of all ages can pledge to pray for vocations
- The children in parish schools, religious education classes, and those in youth ministry write cards of affirmation to the priests
- A reception after Masses is held for parishioners to thank their priests and enjoy fellowship
- Bilingual material is available for the book rack, bulletin, prayer drive, and another reception after a Spanish Mass is offered

These are hypothetical examples of a very robust celebration of Priesthood Sunday—a single day in the life of a parish that has a dedicated Vocation Ministry.

What if efforts like these are sustained year-round, year after year? From my own experience in a typical suburban parish, the results are tremendous! And we are not an isolated example. I have heard from many other parishes with similar ministries. Whether they call themselves the "Vocation Committee," or the "Vocation Task Force," or have creative names like the "Hands of Mary" or "The Vianney Society," the results are very similar. Over time, adults and children in these parishes find that the concept of "vocation" becomes second nature.

An active Vocation Ministry changes the parish in tangible and intangible ways. On the physical level (we Catholics are a sacramental people after all), there is a visible change in the parish. Take the annual seminarian poster, for example. It's not tacked onto a bulletin board in a dark corner of the church foyer. Rather, it's blown up, mounted on foam board or framed, and displayed prominently. In the school, children pass by a life-sized cutout of a priest on a daily basis. In the parish hall, tasteful banners consistently remind people to "Pray for Vocations."

In the ideal vocation-minded parish, the mentality of adults and children is different. Adults not only understand the general concept of vocation—the reality that God calls everyone—but they also have a grasp on how the Church understands the sacraments of Holy Marriage and Holy Orders. How is this achieved? In a hundred different ways: by the priest's educational homilies, through simple things like bulletin blurbs, through more complex activities like panel discussions with seminarians. The children, too, have a developed view of vocations. Thanks to close collaboration with Catholic teachers, catechists, and youth ministers, students of all ages thoroughly understand principles of discernment.

Parishes that have active Vocation Ministries are different on a spiritual level, too. Parents and grandparents will learn more about the joy of living the life God has asked of each person. Eventually, this will help them become vocation promoters in their own homes and be more open to having religious vocations come from their families. They will know how to support their children and grandchildren when they are discerning their vocations. When youth feel the support of their family, they can open their hearts more easily and say yes to God's call.

How to Interact with Discerning Young People

Those working for vocations tend to spot promising young people: those who stay after Mass to pray or are regularly involved serving in the parish. Something just seems different about them. When you do approach that young man or women, and I hope you do, be sensitive to where he or she is on this journey. Teens are like wild animals; they are easy to scare away. Sometimes we can be so excited that we unknowingly pounce on them with eagerness. Instead, approach them carefully.

For example, if you see a prayerful young woman after Mass, you could say something like, "I couldn't help but notice how prayerful you are, and I think you may have some characteristics of a religious sister." If she says, "I've recently started to think about that," tell her that you will pray for her, and if it seems right, give her your contact information.

Likewise, if a young man serves the parish as an altar server, lector, or Extraordinary Minister of Holy Communion, you may say, "I've noticed your reverence during Mass and thought you may make a great priest one day." If he replies that he has been seriously discerning this possibility for some time, then it may be a good opportunity to recommend his reading *To Save a Thousand Souls: A Guide for Discerning a Vocation to Diocesan Priesthood*, which can help him to discover the steps of discernment and where he is in the process. Definitely share your contact information and express that you will pray for him.

In either of the scenarios presented, if the young person expresses disinterest, don't lose heart. You have planted an idea, and in the ideal vocation-minded parish, the Holy Spirit will have many chances to water that seed and let it grow, no matter where it leads.

Support those discerning in your parish by respecting their privacy and giving them space. Pray for them, especially in your monthly meetings, for their continued openness to God's will. Remember, your agenda is not to get as many vocations as possible, but to help young people discern God's will in their lives.

Lastly, if the parish has a young man or woman in formation, either in a religious community or seminary, realize that this is still a time of discernment. Fr. T.J. Dolce, Vocation Director for the Archdiocese of Galveston-Houston, explains that when he entered seminary the process of discernment was not over but actually continued in a more earnest way. He learned more about the Catholic faith and what it means to be a priest.

Be supportive of young men and women, especially if they discern out of formation for the priesthood or religious life. We need to encourage them during what can be a challenging time, thanking them for seeking out God's will in their lives. Ultimately, with the valuable training and education they received, they can become better Catholics and, God willing, husbands or wives.

Personal Ministry Highlight

One of the highlights of my time serving in Vocation Ministry happened when a few teenage girls approached me after a panel of religious sisters and priests spoke at a Life Teen event. They enthusiastically sought me out, asking how they could find out more about particular orders. They were certain they had a calling to religious life.

I shared their enthusiasm and affirmed them for asking God what he wants for their lives and responding to that call with an open heart. Since they were seeking more information, we walked over to the church book rack, where I gave them a Vision Magazine (www.vocationnetwork.org) which would answer some questions and give them some gentle guidance. I also handed them some prayer materials and encouraged them to keep praying in this early stage of the process, being open to God's will.

While this does not happen often, my heart is overcome with joy when it does.

My Own Story

Before we delve too much further into how to form your Vocation Ministry, I should tell you about my own journey. At my home parish, Saint Cecilia in Houston, we stand on the shoulders of giants. Our Parish Vocation Committee (PVC), which was formed in the 1980s, was one of the first in our diocese. Bob Powell, Walter Knaugton, Jim DeNike (former president of Serra US), and others sacrificed greatly to promote and affirm vocations. They were known as pioneers in the work of vocations.

For years, these men and many others promoted vocations to priesthood and religious life with prayer, receptions, and activities for schoolchildren and altar servers.

Eventually when a vacuum of leadership occurred, the once-energetic committee became virtually dormant. The word "vocation" was truly forgotten at our parish.

A few years ago our pastor asked our newly ordained parochial vicar, Father Victor Perez, to revive the committee. My husband David and I, along with about five other parishioners, were asked to attend a meeting with the founding members.

Although I had converted to Catholicism twelve years prior, I did not know what the word vocation meant. But after hearing Father Victor's enthusiasm for the success of this committee at the first meeting, I was hooked!

I went home and researched as much material about promoting vocations as I could. I found several websites with various activities but nothing about how to start or revive a parish-based committee, so we had no guide to follow. Our brand-new, filled-with-the-Holy-Spirit parochial vicar wanted to set our parish on fire for Jesus and place a spotlight on vocations by holding a wide variety of events to increase parishioners' interest in vocations. Most of the time I felt like I was barely keeping my head above water, but I wasn't deterred. This work was too important.

Though there was a huge learning curve for us, I was having the time of my life with the committee. Who knew how much fun this work could be? Whether I was hanging around priests, sisters, or those in formation at a church function, or playing pin-the-miter-on-the-bishop with the children at our parish festival, I was having a blast! Most importantly, I felt like our ministry was making a real difference in the culture of our church.

Early on in our efforts, one of the decisions our group made was to change our name. Being without a Parish Vocation Committee for over five years, we felt the parishioners needed ministering to, so we decided to become a Vocation Ministry. Furthermore, to the average American Catholic, the term "committee" can bring about thoughts like "boring meetings and meaningless work", while "ministry" connotes "prayer and action." This small but meaningful step gave us a mindset of compassion for all our parishioners. Father Victor designed this distinctive logo, which we include on all communications about our ministry.

After naming ourselves, we developed a mission statement that encapsulated all we had determined was important to our ministry:

> *"The goal of the Vocation Ministry is to create a vocations-friendly environment that engages our parish and archdiocesan community and inspires families to encourage, support, and call forth vocations. We will honor and support those already in their vocations, especially our pastor and retired priests. We will spiritually adopt through daily prayer those discerning or already on the path to ordination or final vows."*

My parish is no different than many of yours, with many of the same struggles. At times, we don't have enough money or volunteers for a given activity. We do our part to make sacrifices to be the hands and feet of

Christ. God called me as an unlikely author and speaker on vocations, and I am doing my best to follow his will. We tread our own path and let the Holy Spirit guide our ministry. You will tread yours too, but I hope this book helps make that path easier.

Saint Anthony of Padua was said to be "worn out" doing the work the Lord asked of him before he died. Let us be worn out for Christ, using our gifts to serve his Church.

Patron Saint of Vocations: St. Alphonsus Liguori

S t. Alphonsus Liguori is a powerful intercessor for vocations. He was born near Naples in 1696. As the eldest of seven children, he was seen as the "hope of his house." He did not attend traditional school but was educated by tutors, earning a degree as Doctor of Law at the age of sixteen.

Unfortunately, by the time he was twenty-six, Alphonsus had largely forgotten the faith of his youth and had become enamored with high society. Sometime later, he lost an important case, had his pride broken, and was brought back to God, spending his days praying for God's will in his life.

The answer to his prayers came when he was visiting the ill in the Hospital for Incurables. Surrounded by a mysterious light, he felt the house rocking and an interior voice said, "Leave the world and give thyself to me." This occurred twice. Then and there he laid his sword before the statue of Our Lady and made a solemn promise to enter the ecclesiastical state.

Alphonsus was ordained into the Fathers of the Oratory in 1726 and spent six years holding missions throughout Naples. He founded the Congregation of the Most Holy Redeemer in 1732.

In March 1762, Clement XIII appointed Alphonsus bishop of Saint Agatha of the Goths, a diocese in Southern Italy. Finding more than 30,000 uneducated men and women and 400 priests, he set out instructing families and teaching theology, while reorganizing the seminary and religious houses.

Unfortunately, Alphonsus was not physically well. Rheumatoid arthritis slowly deformed his body to a point that his head became bent forward and he had to be fed with tubes. Finally, an attack of rheumatic fever left him permanently paralyzed.

Despite his many infirmities, both Clement XIII and Clement XIV obliged Alphonsus to remain at his post. He oversaw his congregation until age eighty-six. He died on Aug. 1, 1787 as the midday Angelus was ringing.

In 1839, Alphonsus was canonized, and in 1871, Pius IX declared him a Doctor of the Church, saying, "No less remarkable than the intensity with which Alphonsus worked is the amount of work he did. His perseverance was indomitable. He both made and kept a vow not to lose a single moment of time."

St. Alphonsus is a holy example of using all our time on earth to work for God's Kingdom. St. Alphonsus Liguori, pray for us!

CHAPTER TWO

FOUNDATION & ORGANIZATION

"You want to do something for the Lord—do it. Whatever you feel need to be done, even though you're shaking in your boots, you're scared to death—take the first step forward. The grace comes with that one step and you get the grace as you step. Being afraid is not a problem; it's doing nothing when you're afraid."

These words of wisdom come from the unlikely founder of the world's largest Catholic media network. Born in 1923, Rita Rizzo was a sickly child from a broken home with no religious background. She came of age in the Depression era and did not see a television set until age 38, well after having become a religious sister. Her first television appearance was at age 55. Shortly after, she and the other sisters in her cloistered community turned their monastery garage into a television studio. Suffering physical ailments, severe financial constraints, and even conflicts with Church hierarchy, she persevered in her vision. By age 70, this physically frail but persistent religious sister had established a television network that had become a household name among millions of Catholics. To this day, the Eternal Word Television Network (EWTN) continues to expand its reach worldwide.

Looking back on the network's obstacles and achievements, Mother Angelica was always quick to give credit to God: "Unless you are willing to do the ridiculous, God will not do the miraculous."

Of course, running a Parish Vocation Ministry is smaller in scope than running a global television network.

Nonetheless, the task can seem daunting. What exactly should the ministry do? Who will help? What can the parish afford? Will the pastor be supportive? Am I the right leader? Will our work make a difference?

These and many other questions will arise. But if you feel called by God to promote vocations—if God has truly placed this mission on your heart—then trust the Holy Spirit and take a step forward. Whether starting a new Vocation Ministry or reviving an old one, be open to God's will for the ministry and the parish. Trust in God is the key to success. Trust that it is God who will transform the parish, but that he has called *you* to be his hands and feet.

Prayer is the Foundation

Prayer is foundational for a successful Vocation Ministry. To set the right tone from the very beginning, it's immensely helpful to consecrate the ministry to Mary or another saint (see page 56). Before embarking on this rewarding and challenging journey, the Vocation Ministry should commit every aspect of the ministry to prayer. Any new ministry is bound to have triumphs and frustrations, successes and setbacks, so trust that it is all part of God's plan, and entrust your activities to him.

Members must remain faithful to regular prayer and be open to the prompting of the Holy Spirit. Regardless of the size and complexity of the ministry, keeping focused on the spiritual nature of the work is critical. St. Paul urges the faithful to "pray without ceasing" (1 Thessalonians 5:17). Include the work of vocations into that unending petition to God.

For what should you pray? Pray for what God has planned for the ministry. Pray for your parish priests. Pray that God will call the right volunteers to participate, and pray that God will use the ministry to touch hearts and inspire vocations. Furthermore, pray for God to provide the resources for the ministry to accomplish its goals. No task is too large for God. He will make it happen if he wills it.

Ask the Blessed Mother to pray for the ministry, as well. She was the first disciple of Jesus. Ask the patron saints of vocations, such as Saint Alphonsus Liguori and Saint Junípero Serra, for their intercessory prayers.

Finally, ask other faithful parishioners to pray for the mission of the ministry.

At my home parish, our ministry has several members who cannot physically help at our activities throughout the year. One such member is a consecrated virgin who must live apart from her community to take care of her elderly mother in another city.

She receives the ministry emails and keeps all of our members and activities in her prayers. I am quite certain that one of the reasons our activities have been successful are her prayers and sacrifices for our ministry.

Jesus gave advice to his disciples that rings true for all: "Have faith in God. Amen, I say to you, whoever says to this mountain, 'Be lifted up and thrown into the sea,' and does not doubt in his heart but believes that what he says will happen, it shall be done for him. Therefore I tell you, all that you ask for in prayer, believe that you will receive it and it shall be yours" (Mark 11:23-25).

Believe that vocations can spring forth with dedication and prayer from each parish and that the Church and all Catholics will receive the graces that come from having more religious sisters and brothers, more priests, and more sacramental marriages. Pray without ceasing!

Membership in Your Vocation Ministry

As with any organization, having the right people involved is key. Every ministry must have the support of a pastor or priest in order to proceed with confidence and effectiveness. To help things run smoothly, the ministry needs a faithful, perceptive director. As the ministry grows, it will add new members with different strengths, interests, and personalities. Each ministry will need to adapt to the parish it is serving, of course, but the basic personnel roles are similar. The following sections examine some key roles.

Priest

As shepherd of his flock, the priest provides the Vocation Ministry with vision, direction, advice, and ideas that can only come from a priest's perspective. His vantage point allows him to see the entire parish—its needs, its activities, and its direction.

His role in the ministry will be vital, no matter what form it takes. He could be somewhat removed from the day-to-day operations, meeting with the director monthly, quarterly, or semi-annually to make sure the ministry is on the right path. In some parishes, the priest may decide to take a more active role, attending meetings and events on a regular basis and fully engaging in discussions and planning. Most priests' involvement will lie somewhere between these two scenarios.

Be prayerful, kind, and understanding about how busy and exhausting a priest's life can be. Realistically a priest, especially a pastor, is likely to take an advisory role within the ministry, and that is generally what is needed most. If the priest cannot regularly participate, he may ask another priest, a deacon, or a religious brother or sister to be his representative at the meetings.

Having a priest or pastor champion the work the Vocation Ministry is something to be treasured. They will lend the ministry credibility and visibility, not to mention knowledge and wisdom. If a priest is not personally involved in the ministry, it is a worthy cause for prayer. If such a champion does arise, the ministry should work diligently to affirm him throughout the year. Take his advice seriously and with humility and open-mindedness, knowing that he has the parish's best intentions in mind.

Personal Ministry Highlight

Father Victor Perez, at the time our new parochial vicar, invited me to my first vocation meeting. He was a true champion for our ministry. He has a heart for Jesus Christ, our Blessed Mother Mary, and vocations. He always made time for our meetings and attended most of our ministry activities, inspiring all those with whom he came into contact.

Fr. Victor viewed vocation work as an important way of serving Christ, who is ultimately the one calling. He taught us to pray for vocations through the consecration prayer he wrote, and by being a witness of prayer. He was seen in Eucharistic adoration daily. He showed us how to immerse our work and activities in prayer, especially asking for the prayers of our Blessed Mother, the mother and model of vocations, knowing she would always point us to Christ.

We had a wonderful working relationship that allowed me to seek his advice on all minor and major events. When we wanted to invite seminarians, sisters, or other priests to take part in an activity, Father Victor would personally call them. If our ministry sought to interact with the parish school children, normally for National Vocation Awareness Week, he would meet with the principal of the school. Rarely did anyone say no to him.

He paved the way for our ministry to make great strides in our mission of making Saint Cecilia Catholic Church a vocation-minded parish. At our parish festival, he was not afraid to look silly when arm-wrestling the children or participating in a hula-hoop contest. Parishioners could see his joy in being a priest. Most importantly, Father Victor taught us how to make prayer a central goal of our ministry. He exuded the Holy Spirit and attracted many faith-filled parishioners to our ministry.

Ministry Director

For a ministry to succeed, it must have a dedicated leader who is willing to share his or her abilities, time, and passion for vocations. This sacrifice is always rewarded by God. As St. Paul tells us: "God, who will repay everyone according to his works: eternal life to those who seek glory, honor, and immortality through perseverance in good works ... Let us not grow tired of doing good, for in due time we shall reap our harvest, if we do not give up" (Rom. 2: 5-7; Gal. 6:9-10).

Just as every Vocation Ministry will differ, so too will every director. Some directors will be hands-on; for others, delegation will be a strength. The following are some of the traits that a director may have that will help the ministry thrive.

- **Enthusiasm:** Having exuberance for vocations will attract others to participate as ministry members.

- **Perseverance:** Obstacles will occur often when doing God's work. Knowing and accepting this will keep the Vocation Ministry on track amidst difficulties.
- **Organization:** A Vocation Ministry has a great number of moving parts—people with whom to coordinate, plans, details, activities, ideas, and finances. The director needs to keep everything and everyone rolling in the envisioned direction.
- **Delegation:** Directors who try to do everything themselves not only will suffer burnout, but also will lose the interest and support of ministry members who want to be involved in a meaningful way with assignments and areas of responsibility.
- **Inspiration:** Encouraging others to do their best to be Christ's hands and feet in the parish will keep members excited about the work for years to come.

Another idea that has worked in some parishes is to split the director's job into two co-director positions so that even if one person's life becomes hectic, or the work too burdensome, at least one leader will be able to make meetings and events. Each ministry must do what is best for its own set of members.

Whenever possible, ministry participants should share the load so the director does not become overloaded with too many details. It is incumbent upon the leader to delegate and encourage members to take responsibility for a specific aspect of the ministry, such as an annual event. Clearly defining roles, creating systems of accountability for outcomes, and encouraging and supporting one another will create a ministry that volunteers want to join, and one that produces fruit within the parish.

Youth Minister

A survey of new priests from the class of 2012 indicated that 53 percent participated in a parish youth group when they were in middle and high school.[5]

With that statistic in mind, it makes sense that whenever possible the youth minister should be an active member of the Vocation Ministry.

5 "New Priests Younger, Were Altar Servers, Lectors, Carry Debt." www.USCCB.org

Teens and pre-teens are the most likely parishioners to be contemplating their futures. Youth ministers are in regular contact with youth and understand how they think. Their unique perspective will be invaluable in choosing and planning events that will make the biggest impact on the youth of the parish.

The director should make an appointment with the youth minister to discuss ways the two ministries can work together to promote vocations in the parish. If the youth minister is not immediately open to collaboration, pray and offer to support him or her in every way possible.

Other Ministry Members

For all of the ways Vocation Ministries differ from parish to parish, one commonality in every thriving ministry is a group of dedicated, involved volunteers. With only a priest and director, it is impossible to envision, plan, execute, and implement the number and type of activities that create a vocations-rich environment in a parish.

Leaders and followers alike are needed in this work. Ideally, a Vocation Ministry will have a good number of members involved in an assortment of other committees or ministries such as the Knights of Columbus, the young adult group, and those who work with youth in various capacities. When forming or expanding a Vocation Ministry, cast a wide net and specifically look for people who bring different strengths, talents, languages, connections, and experiences—and above all, a heart for vocations.

Whether recruiting for the first time or expanding the ministry, a Vocation Ministry leader should pray that the people whom God has called to work toward encouraging vocations will respond willingly. The ideal candidates are parishioners who are willing to work hard to build up the Kingdom. Strong participants need only love for Jesus our great High Priest, dedication to the Catholic Church, honor for our Blessed Mother whose "Yes" is an example to us all, and a willingness to work diligently to promote vocations.

Recruitment

The current members of the ministry should strive to find individuals from different parts of community life, who come to church often and inspire others to holiness. Diversity in age, gender, background, and ethnicity will enrich and strengthen the ministry by providing opportunities to hear and consider many perspectives. It takes a team, wielding different skills and gifts, to successfully build and coordinate a Vocation Ministry.

When possible recruit bilingual members who can express the specific needs of their cross-section of the community, help communicate the works of the ministry to that population, and execute activities for those parishioners.

Regardless of how many members the ministry has, the recruitment for additional members is never finished. It must be an ongoing process for a number of reasons, not least of which is the fact that recruiting members is the precursor to recruiting for vocations itself. The more people on fire for vocations, the faster the fire will spread to all reaches of the parish and diocese. When more ministry members are available, additional and more complex activities can be implemented, which increases the understanding of vocations in the parish and nudges more hearts toward discernment. When approaching a potential volunteer one-on-one or during a ministry fair, it helps to explain the main focus of the ministry: praying for, affirming, and bringing awareness to vocations. It is important to explain that, while members have fun together planning and executing various activities, it is a working ministry. The recruiting ministry member can explain that volunteers are critical in accomplishing all the work of the ministry. Also, explain that being a part of this ministry is like running a marathon, not a sprint. The activities and events are continuous. Some years are not as hectic as others, but elbow grease is required by all members at some point.

Some parishes have a ministry fair (see activity on page 102), sometimes known as a stewardship fair, to highlight all the ways in which parishioners can become involved in church activities. Normally, after all Masses on a designated weekend, parishioners are invited to a fair that features all the ministries on campus. Parishioners may then discern to which ministry they would like to give their time, talent, and treasure.

All help is needed and should be welcomed. Even if the ministry only gains a few members but speaks to twenty parishioners about what the term "vocation" means, the efforts have been fruitful.

Member Retention

The ministry is a dynamic organization composed of people who both give and need support. The director should do everything possible to nurture members: encouraging them to get involved at a deeper level when the time is right, empowering them to take ownership of an activity or task, and then giving them credit for a job well done. This "member development" keeps these volunteers engaged, appreciated, and active. The most meaningful ministries will allow members to find the areas they are passionate about and best suit their talents and gifts.

The Vocation Ministry members also should give one another personal support. By being there for one another in life—celebrating birthdays or the birth of a child, mourning with a member when he or she has lost a loved one—the ministry will grow in charity through these experiences and will help all participants feel appreciated and encouraged.

The extra effort spent cultivating this sense of camaraderie will result in retention of volunteers for many years and will keep politics and personal agendas to a minimum. Teamwork is needed on all levels of ministry work, and the more friendships that are formed, the more members will naturally stay involved.

Ongoing Formation

A Vocation Ministry can operate more efficiently if members are well educated on all aspects of vocations. Valuable resources exist in print and online. Making these available at meetings can increase effectiveness at the developmental phase, when new members are added, and when a longtime ministry is looking to re-energize its efforts. It would be beneficial to spend 10-15 minutes during each meeting discussing some aspect of vocations. For example, when planning for National Vocation Awareness Week, the ministry could discuss key aspects of each vocation or study some documents ·on vocations. This ongoing formation ensures each member is informed and carrying the same message to the parish.

Another idea for continued formation is for the ministry to go on an annual retreat with a spiritual director. One ministry in Omaha found this was a wonderful way to bring the ministry together not only to formulate the year's vocation plan, but also to inspire the members to continue personal and ministerial growth in the church.

Personal Ministry Highlight

We started our ministry with four or five members personally recruited by our priest. Now we have twenty members with an average of ten to fifteen attendees at each meeting, which gives each person the opportunity to be heard and contribute in a real way.

Our ministry includes our pastor and parochial vicar, two deacons, a consecrated virgin, and several who are married. We have young members and members who are retired.

Some of our members speak Spanish to represent those in our community who do not speak English. Our diversity makes us stronger and better able to think of new events and activities that appeal to all parishioners.

I believe God brought to us people who are meant to be involved with this important work in our parish.

Often, new members found their way to us through various activities and relationships with current members. Sometimes they come from unlikely places or from suggestions. We welcome them all and allow them as much time as needed to find out where their gifts can best be shared. Our members are encouraged to help with a variety of activities, as liaisons, coordinators or workers, whenever they can.

Administrative Aspects

For the ministry to run smoothly, many administrative tasks must be handled efficiently. The director will usually manage these tasks, unless a gifted organizer within the group can help.

The number and level of details required in a growing, active Vocation Ministry can seem overwhelming: keeping track of schedules, meeting agendas, notes, action items, ministry contact information, and emails; communicating with the parish office; communicating with people outside of the parish, such as Serrans, Knights of Columbus, the rector of local seminary, and the principal of parish school; booking rooms within the parish facilities for meetings and activities; and much more. The list goes on and on, which is why the ability to delegate is a desired trait in a ministry director.

Various duties depend on the specific activities of the ministry, but some are required to maintain the day-to-day functions of the ministry itself, such as recruiting and assisting members, preparing for and conducting effective meetings, and developing and tracking the budget. The more these aspects of the work are streamlined and structured, the more time and energy can be devoted to the vocations activities.

Assembling the right team to handle administrative details like planning, scheduling, budgeting, meetings, agendas, and record keeping is important to the success of the ministry. While creating a nurturing environment for vocations is the goal, taking care of the details of the ministry itself will help ensure the continuity of the Vocation Ministry over time.

Meetings

Meetings, while necessary, are not always the most popular activities. However, well-run meetings facilitate a host of important outcomes. They serve to impart news of upcoming events, recap recent events, keep everybody on the same page, foster new ideas, encourage members in their individual endeavors, and build friendships.

Another important facet of Vocation Ministry meetings is remaining positive and grateful for the gifts that everyone brings to this ministry. It is important to celebrate great ideas and significant results. An air of excitement will permeate meetings when everyone hears how God is using their efforts to build up his Church, one activity and prayer at a time. The ministry will be more effective if all members pray together and share a passion for vocations and a love for all parishioners.

The most important advice for the group's leader is to remain open to the guidance of the Holy Spirit.

Being open to new ideas from wherever they may come is a key to effective leadership.

Personal Ministry Highlight

At one meeting, the group was discussing a topic when Father Victor interrupted to say he felt strongly that we needed to pray for our seminarians.

He was impassioned and emphatic that they were under spiritual attack in the seminary and felt we needed to pray for them during this time of formation.

Within two weeks, one of our members and I were meeting with the rector of Saint Mary's Seminary, discussing Father Victor's idea. That discussion evolved into the Spiritual Adoption Program (see page 84).

I spend a few moments in prayer before every meeting asking that everyone, including myself, will remain open to new ideas and the prompting of the Holy Spirit.

The prayer can be simple: "Come Holy Spirit, fill the hearts of your faithful and kindle in them the fire of your love. Send forth your Spirit and they shall be created. And You shall renew the face of the earth."

To provide consistency, schedule meetings monthly on the same day, time, and place so members can plan ahead. To liven things up, the ministry might meet in an interesting location at the parish—perhaps in the youth room or in a room with windows with a garden view. Consider asking members to rotate bringing snacks or a meal from time to time. Remember to do whatever will best promote fellowship among the members.

A sample agenda might look like this:

Introductions
Opening Prayer of Consecration (see page 56)
News/Recap of Recent Events
Upcoming Parish Events
New Ideas
Upcoming Diocesan Events
Prayer List
Prayer for Discerners

Prayer for Discerners
O God, Father of all Mercies,
Provider of a bountiful Harvest, send Your Graces upon those
You have called to gather the fruits of Your labor;
preserve and strengthen them in their lifelong service of you.

Open the hearts of Your children, especially (*names of discerners*)
that they may discern Your Holy Will;
inspire in them a love and desire to surrender themselves
to serving others in the name of Your son, Jesus Christ.

Teach all Your faithful to follow their respective paths in life
guided by Your Divine Word and Truth.
Through the intercession of the Most Blessed Virgin Mary,
all the Angels and Saints, humbly hear our prayers
and grant Your Church's needs, through Christ, our Lord. Amen.[6]

Lastly, at each meeting recap the activities of the prior month to discuss the successes and challenges encountered. Then, decide if the ministry would like to repeat the activity yearly, every few years, or not again. Progress through the stages purposefully, selecting those activities that will resound in the parish halls and through the homes of each parishioner.

---

6 "Prayer for Vocations | Prayer Resources | Faith | Marquette ..." www.marquette.edu. N.p., n.d. Web. 16 Feb. 2014.

Finances

The Vocation Ministry is an investment in a future full of holy priests, religious men and women, and happy marriages. The long-term payoff will be tremendous since the Holy Spirit is in control.

At the beginning, the ministry may choose to focus solely on prayer, which costs no money but produces untold fruit. If the Vocation Ministry opts to do more than pray, it will need to be even more creative in executing certain activities. Some of the least expensive events can have the most influence, such as a prayer drive, a classroom visit from a religious sister, or a Family Holy Hour. Even if the ministry focuses on these simple but powerful activities, the impact could be significant. The best advice is to focus on wherever seeds of holiness can be planted.

For a Vocation Ministry operating in a small parish, the principle of the work is the same: if the parish is more vocation-minded, the Holy Spirit can inspire more families and youth. Even though the parish is small, the activities are not less effective.

I imagine that being in a small parish where most people know each other, the activities could bring the entire parish along for the ride. For example, a pot-luck supper to celebrate the pastor's birthday can be organized with a few phone calls. Forming a prayer chain for seminarians can be done in a snap. Also, don't forget to check with your diocesan Office of Vocations to see which programs they offer that the ministry could promote, cutting down on the costs of hosting similar activities at the parish level.

If your ministry is part of a sizable parish, you may have more volunteers and/or monetary resources with which to work, but the ministry will still need to assess what it can realistically achieve.

Keep in mind that the activities may be done on a grander scale, but that does not always translate into greater effectiveness. Sometimes a well-written announcement before or after Masses can be just as effective as a beautiful but costly banner. On the other hand, flowers, invitations, and catering make a big difference at an ordination anniversary reception.

Having a larger parish can present its own challenges. Here are some suggestions for larger parishes. First, when organizing parish-wide events that can draw hundreds of parishioners, draw on volunteers and funds from other ministries at the parish. Second, word of mouth may not be as effective for publicity, so employ other forms of media such as your website and e-newsletter. Third, gaining an identity as a ministry may take longer, so consider adding a logo to all promotional material.

The size of the parish does not always guarantee wealth either, so if the church can afford little or no financial support, look at all fundraising options. Consider holding a raffle or selling *"We Love Our Priests"* buttons before Masses on Priesthood Sunday.

From personal experience, parishioners tend to be extremely generous when they realize their money is going toward vocations. Ask the pastor if a donation box can be placed at activities so that parishioners can donate to this worthy cause. Moreover, other organizations or groups might help fund an endeavor which will bring others into the mission of the ministry. Keep all ideas for funding on the table.

When budgeting, be mindful that each parish has a date by which budgets must be submitted to the parish administrator. The ministry director must keep records of the activities in the first year or up until that first budget due date. In future years, budgets are often built on the previous year's expenditures so new, larger requests should be accompanied by justification. Define as clearly as possible which activities the Vocation Ministry will pursue the following year. Anticipate some cost increases, even if the activity has been done in the past (see sample budgets in Appendix A).

Work closely with benefactors and volunteers who pay for things up front with anticipation of being reimbursed. All purchases should be pre-approved and receipts received immediately for reimbursement. When receipts are not collected in a timely manner or a purchase is not approved beforehand, bad feelings can occur resulting in the loss of valuable members and resources. Moreover, it is important to account for all expenditures, even those made with donated funds. There may come a day when a vital donor no longer chooses to donate or is no longer a member of the parish, and recreating those events without full financial support will require funding from other sources.

While struggling to find funds to start and build EWTN, Mother Angelica said, "Money is his problem. Working for his Kingdom is mine... he takes care of his problem, and I take care of mine."[7]

---

7 Arroyo, Raymond. "Mother Angelica"

Whether beginning a ministry or trying to expand activities, the ministry should focus on doing whatever the Holy Spirit inspires it to do, and the generous Lord will provide the means to accomplish the work.

Partners in Vocation Ministry

Various groups and organizations throughout each diocese are working toward the goal of vocation awareness. If they will labor together in a coordinated effort, the harvest will be plentiful. Each ministry should prayerfully consider collaborating with groups that have similar goals.

Office of Vocations

Each diocese has a special office that is charged with promoting and fostering vocations to the priesthood. Some of these offices also promote religious life. Reaching out and joining forces with your diocesan Office of Vocations should be among the first steps for a new Vocation Ministry.

For an established ministry, ongoing collaboration with this office is important. The staff members in these offices welcome the help from parish-based volunteers.

Moreover, when reaching out to the Office of Vocations, find out specifically how your Vocation Ministry can help them at your parish. For example, they may need each ministry to promote their discernment events. They also may have a special prayer card for vocations that they would rather all parishes use. Ask if the Vocation Director might be willing to do a presentation or workshop for your parish school, after Masses, or for your ministry.

The Office of Vocations maintains a website that can educate a ministry on certain aspects of vocations, including seminary studies and discernment opportunities for the priesthood and religious life, among various other topics. For example, www.houstonvocations.com offers videos of priests and sisters explaining different parts of the discernment process, as well as articles written by seminarians about their experience in the seminary.

Personal Ministry Highlight

A few of our ministry members visited our Office of Vocations within the first six months of our initial meeting. We were on fire for all things vocations, and we wanted to meet those specifically in charge of vocation events for our archdiocese. They were extremely welcoming. We shared with them the ministry events at Saint Cecilia and walked away inspired to do even more.

We found it helpful to learn more about the activities offered through our Office of Vocations such as Come and See weekends, where young men visit a seminary and young women visit a convent.

We discovered that, along with the seminarian poster, there is also a poster of consecrated men and women in formation which are given to each parish and school. We were also given some tools such as brochures and prayer cards to help us in our work. The staff could not have been more thrilled to hear that our ministry members were praying for and promoting vocations.

Serra Club

Named after Saint Junípero Serra, the Serra Club is an international organization devoted to the promotion of vocations to the priesthood and religious life. Founded in Seattle in the 1930s, Serra International now has more than eight hundred clubs in thirty-seven countries, with a total membership of more than nineteen thousand men and women.

Serra Clubs have regular meetings during which they pray specifically for vocations. They coordinate a wide range of programs in parishes, schools, and dioceses.

These clubs are a valuable resource for any Vocation Ministry, new or established. At www.serraus.org, Vocation Ministries can find the nearest club, as well as ideas designed by Serra to encourage, affirm, and promote vocations.

Personal Ministry Highlight

Our parish had a special opportunity to visit with the Serra Club of Northwest Houston, whose members have prayed for, promoted, and affirmed vocations for many years. The club president asked our parochial vicar, Father Victor Perez, to give his vocation testimony and tell them about our ministry. We shared a meal and many stories, prayed a rosary for vocations, and heard Father Victor's incredibly inspiring vocation testimony.

Our ministry was humbled to be with so many who have been on the front lines for vocations for decades. These Serrans offer a wealth of knowledge and support, and they could not have been more encouraging of the work we were doing at Saint Cecilia.

Knights of Columbus

In the late 19th century, Father Michael McGivney, a Connecticut parish priest, founded the Knights of Columbus, now the world's largest Catholic fraternal service organization with more than 1.8 million members in fourteen thousand local councils. The Knights are strong supporters of vocations. They donate millions of dollars to seminarians through their RSVP program and also provide vocation-related resources to each council. They can be valuable collaborators with your ministry at the parish level.

In both new and established ministries, the ministry leader or parish priest should request the involvement of the Knights of Columbus so their energies can be combined to promote vocations.

If there is not a Knights of Columbus council at your parish, search www.kofc.org to find one nearby.

Personal Ministry Highlight

We were not even a ministry for a few months before discovering that a young man who graduated from our parish school and belonged to our parish was going to be ordained that next June. We had only three months to coordinate an ordination reception that he would remember for a lifetime.

Enter the Knights of Columbus, who always answered our pleas for help! We asked them to serve food for the reception, and they were thrilled to be of assistance. They also gave the new priest a beautiful chalice as a present. I am so grateful to God that in his perfect timing our ministry was in existence to affirm this man and to show our parishioners this newly ordained priest's joy!

The Knights of Columbus have now helped our ministry countless times by donating manpower and funds needed for various projects. They donated and handed out over 1,000 rosary rings after all Masses for World Day of Prayer for Vocations.

Youth Ministry

Katie Hartfiel is a former youth minister and a nationally-known speaker who wrote the book *Woman in Love*. She says:

"Teens want to be challenged to be heroic, and they are ready for that challenge. So often we encourage them to be heroic in sports and academics, but we do not need to be afraid of challenging them to be heroic in their faith. When we teach them how to search for God's guidance in the decisions in their lives, whether it be where to attend college or what activities they should be involved with, they become accustomed to saying 'Yes' to God, so when he calls the big call, that vocations call, they are ready."

By involving the youth, a Vocation Ministry can encourage the children, teens, and young adults to be much more receptive to God's call to holiness and to their vocation. For example, on Priesthood Sunday, the priest's birthday, or his ordination anniversary, the ministry could ask the youth to sign a card or remind them to send "happy birthday" emails to the priest.

This simple task helps foster an appreciation for the priesthood among the teens.

The Vocation Ministry can help the youth minister in a number of ways:

- Share vocation materials, such as seminarian posters and prayer cards (see page 64).
- Offer to help host a vocation night once a year, where a panel of religious sisters and brothers, priests, and/or married couples reveal their vocation testimony with the teens.
- Organize a tour of the closest seminary for the boys.

Teens, in turn, can help the Vocation Ministry at events in the following ways:

- Help set up for receptions (see page 189).
- Make rosaries to include with the Traveling Vocations Chalice Program (see page 72) that the family can use during the week and possibly keep as a gift.
- Participate in tug-of-war and other games at your parish festival (see page 100).
- Make posters to advertise events or to say "Happy Birthday, Father John!" or "Happy Priesthood Sunday!" (see activity on page 166).
- Pass out prayer cards or rosary rings after Masses.

A Vocation Ministry that lays down a foundation of prayer and adds dedicated members and partners will set the stage for a thriving vocation-minded parish.

Saint Junípero Serra

Saint Junípero Serra, for whom the Serra Club is named, is another great intercessor for vocation efforts.

Born Miguel Jose Serra on Spain's island of Mallorca in 1713, Serra entered the Franciscan Order, taking the name of Saint Francis' childlike companion, Brother Juniper.

"Until he was 35, he spent most of his time in the classroom—first as a student of theology and then as a professor. He also became famous for his preaching. Suddenly he gave it all up and followed the yearning that had begun years before when he heard about the missionary work of St. Francis Solanus in South America. Junipero's desire was to convert native peoples in the New World."[8]

He arrived in Mexico City in 1750 and was assigned to the Sierra Gorda region, where he worked among the Pame Indians. He then spent another eight years preaching across central Mexico. In 1768, at the age of 55, Father Serra took over the missions of the Jesuits in the Mexican provinces of Lower California and Upper California which form modern-day California.

An indefatigable worker and dedicated missionary, Serra was in large part responsible for the foundation and spread of the Church on the West Coast of the United States when it was still mission territory. He traveled thousands of miles on foot, personally established nine missions including present-day San Diego, and supervised the Franciscans who founded twelve more missions. He converted thousands of Native Americans, teaching them sound methods of agriculture, cattle raising, and arts and crafts.

In August 1784, worn out by his apostolic labors, Father Serra was called to his eternal rest. He was beatified by Pope John Paul II in 1988 and his date of canonization was set for September 23, 2015 by Pope Francis. His feast day is July 1.

---

8 Foley, Leonard, O.F.M. "Blessed Junipero Serra"" www.AmericanCatholic.org. N.p., n.d. Web. 27 Jan. 2015.

CHAPTER THREE

PHASES OF A VOCATION MINISTRY

W orking within a Catholic parish can be very rewarding. But as any long-term volunteer knows, poorly-organized efforts can be frustrating. A typical church committee suffers from a variety of troubles:

- Frequent transitions in leaders and committee members
- Subsequent loss of knowledge because of turnover
- Jumping into the deep end with activities that the ministry is not prepared for—and drowning
- Repetitive activities becoming stale
- Loss of volunteer interest
- Not having a written plan to follow

To avoid these common pitfalls in a Vocation Ministry, especially a new one, it is absolutely critical to understand the ministry's developmental stages, or what we call "phases." The importance of the concept of phases cannot be overstated. Similar to a weekend athlete overextending himself and suffering an injury, a Vocation Ministry risks biting off more than it can chew and subsequently suffering a setback with far-reaching implications. Pay careful attention to this section on phases, and use the experience-based advice on how to choose the most appropriate activities at fitting times.

The point of the phases is to implement activities in an order that the ministry's human and financial resources can handle and that the parish is prepared to receive. Achieving success with smaller, simpler, but meaningful activities before tackling the larger, more expensive, and more complex ones will keep attitudes in the ministry and parish positive. Alternatively, presenting an activity that requires a long-term commitment to a parish that has minimal understanding of vocations may leave a bad impression of the concept and the ministry.

The first step in planning the ministry's pursuits is to take inventory of the parish by asking a few important questions:

- To what degree does the parish understand the concept of vocation?
- To what extent is the parish—including priests, adults, youth ministry, and the parish school—ready to promote vocations?
- How much can the ministry handle in its current phase of development?
- How much manpower and money are available?
- Which activities will be implemented and when?

It is critical to thoroughly consider and analyze each aspect of a ministry before holding any activities. The launch or growth of a ministry requires prudence and strategy to be successful. The last obstacle any Vocation Ministry needs is internal resistance or a reputation for overreaching or being disorganized in its efforts. Sensible planning and logical execution will minimize the avoidable issues.

Every parish is different, and every ministry is different, so don't feel overly constrained by the phase labels. These phases are not rigid; they are a guide to help a ministry decide when to tackle activities. We must leave room for the Holy Spirit to inspire each ministry to do what is best for its parish.

Pre-launch: Preparing to Serve

The earliest stage of a ministry is pre-launch, when the ministry is essentially an idea or a vision. In some cases, the priest has approached a parishioner about leading the ministry.

This is a positive scenario, because it means the priest is fully engaged and has put a high priority on promoting vocations in the parish. Such support will be instrumental in the ministry's success. Another scenario is when a parishioner feels called to start or re-energize a Vocation Ministry.

The first step for the parishioner is to pray. In the Gospel of Luke, the Lord calls his followers to ask for vocations, and prayer opens the heart of individuals to God's calling, even those who have not yet responded (c.f. Luke 10:2). Prayer "plows the field," so that seeds will have fertile ground in which to grow in the vineyard of the Lord.

The potential ministry director should meet with the pastor or priest who would have administrative authority over the ministry, to share the plan for bringing about a more vocation-minded parish. It is important to receive the priest's blessing before initiating any activity at the parish or involving more parishioners.

For individuals who have never spoken one-on-one with the parish priest, this meeting could be somewhat intimidating. Here are some valuable tips to make that initial meeting a success:

- **Be humble.** It is easy to be swept up in the excitement of Vocation Ministry work! Remember that regardless of how much research has been done to prepare for the meeting, there is much more to learn. Speak respectfully of any efforts that may have come before this new endeavor and listen intently to feedback from the priest.

- **Keep it simple.** When presenting ideas for starting the ministry, pick a few initiatives that require no funding and few, if any, volunteers. Convey the simplicity of these activities to the priest. This makes it as easy as possible for him to say, "Yes." Start with something relatively easy like, "I would like to ask our parishioners to pray for vocations."

- **Convey that the Vocation Ministry will work hard to encourage, educate, and promote vocations.** Let him know that the goal is for a group of volunteers to perform the tasks involved in the ministry, under his general or direct guidance, and that impact on the staff will be minimal.

- **Ask for his ideas and permission.** If the pastor or priest seems to be supportive, speak to him about his ideas for the ministry and ask his permission to form a small ministry to brainstorm other ways to affirm and promote vocations. Once he gives his blessing, the ministry can move ahead.
- **Offer an alternative.** If he does not support the idea at this time, respect that decision and ask permission to place vocation material in the book rack or to have some other minimally invasive activity like leaving prayer cards for vocations on the tables at the back of church for World Day of Prayer for Vocations. Keep the request reasonable and simple. If he says, "Yes," show that you can execute the simple tasks and keep praying. After a few months, meet with him again or ask him at a convenient time if blurbs encouraging vocations can be placed in the parish bulletin. Keep praying for the priest, for the ministry, and for God to bring life and energy to vocation awareness in the parish.

A third scenario involves gathering parishioners who would like to join the Vocation Ministry effort, then meeting with the priest. This enables the acting director to show the priest that a dedicated group is ready to work to encourage vocations in the parish. This option should be pursued with caution, however, as not all pastors or priests will be open to this approach.

Once the priest and ministry director are on the same page, they likely will decide on a name for the ministry group, typically Parish Vocation Committee or Vocation Ministry, and begin praying about the needs of the parish. At that point, the director should proceed as the priest has recommended and start assembling members who will share in the vision for a more vocation-minded parish.

Phase I: Laying the Groundwork

Now the fun begins! It is time to start thinking about the activities the Vocation Ministry will implement within the next year. For any event hosted by the Vocation Ministry, the ministry needs to start praying early that God will bring together the needed people, ideas, and resources to make the event successful and allow it to glorify him.

A ministry in Phase I is either young in its maturity or is serving a parish that is very early in its growth toward supporting vocations. In either case, the most appropriate activities are those that require few resources—no funding, little in the way of manpower and organization— and serve mostly to raise vocations awareness. Such a ministry is likely focused on basic prayer activities, bulletin blurbs and book rack material, and affirming their priests.

The activities in this phase are vitally important for the early and long-term success of a Vocation Ministry and the peace, energy, and joy of the volunteers involved. Also, some activities in the early phases should continue throughout the work of the ministry, akin to a sports team that regularly practices fundamentals. For example, praying for vocations either after daily Mass or during Eucharistic adoration should occur throughout the work of the ministry. The activities of Phase I are the foundation upon which all other activities are laid. For that reason, ministries in every stage of development are strongly encouraged to include them in their annual plan.

Lastly, in each phase, a list of possible ministry roles is included. For some parishes, having a director and one or two volunteers will be significant progress. In that case, roles may be fluid and less formally defined. Other ministries may be blessed with a number of individuals with a passion for vocations. Having clear roles will help not only keep the ministry functioning smoothly but also will keep the volunteers motivated. In every case, allowing volunteers time to discover and offer their gifts and services will strengthen both the ministry and the members.

Possible Ministry Positions in Phase I

- **Ministry Head** (pastor or priest): Guides the ministry and provides approval as necessary; meets regularly with the ministry director to plan meetings or provide general direction; serves as liaison for clergy. (Note: This is the only position in Phase I filled by a paid member of the parish staff. All others are filled by volunteers.)

- **Ministry Director:** Leads the ministry in day-to-day functions; meets with the ministry head to plan monthly meetings; plans, coordinates, and facilitates meetings; recruits and organizes volunteers; coordinates with the ministry head; budgets the ministry finances, including keeping track of expenses and donations; often plans and coordinates specific ministry activities.
- **Affirmation Coordinator:** Fulfills specific duties such as obtaining greeting cards and putting together care packages for the parish priests; affirming priests, religious, and married couples in the parish.
- **Communications Coordinator:** Writes and submits vocations blurbs and event promotions for the weekly bulletin and any other avenues of publicity, including websites and newsletters; coordinates ordering and printing any materials, such as prayer cards, posters, banners, and promotional material.
- **Spanish-Speaking Representative:** Communicates all ministry programs with the Spanish-speaking community; helps the ministry provide bilingual activities; recommends vocation programs for the Spanish-speaking community.

Phase II: Establishing a Presence

While God inspires all vocations, programs and activities can invite and encourage individuals to be open to God's call. Phase II activities are designed to establish a ministry's strong presence among both adults and youth within the parish.

During this phase, a ministry focuses on asking parishioners to pray for vocations and increases awareness of vocations among youth and all parishioners at special events such as a fall festival. The ministry should also begin to affirm the pastor and priests on a slightly larger scale than was done in Phase I.

A ministry in Phase II continues to have a strong foundation of prayer and is open to the direction of the Holy Spirit in deciding which direction to go next. No idea is too small or large, so allow the members of the ministry and the clergy many opportunities to provide input.

A ministry could stay in Phase II for years due to the number and depth of the activities offered.

There is no timetable for the phases. Each ministry must do what is best for its parish before moving onto the next phase.

The tasks in Phase II are more involved, so some of the suggested positions may be filled by more than one volunteer. Some high-energy volunteers may hold several of the positions, and some may not hold a formal position but may support a coordinator or the director by performing specific tasks. Every person's contribution is valuable.

Possible Ministry Positions in Phase II

- See positions from Phase I.
- **Adoration for Vocations Coordinator:** Coordinates Eucharistic adoration for vocations.
- **School Liaison:** Works with the school to execute activities that promote vocations.
- **Parish Festival Coordinator:** Responsible for the ministry booth at annual parish festival.
- **Special Events Coordinator:** Responsible for organizing parish events supporting vocations, including receptions.

Phase III: Spreading the Word

After establishing a solid foundation of prayer and education in the parish, a ministry in Phase III is typically well-established and running smoothly. Positive changes are occurring within the parish, and more parishioners recognize and affirm the work. The ministry is ready for even more transformative activities, including spreading the good word of vocations outside of the parish. Even with the growth in maturity, a ministry is strongly encouraged to continue praying and asking for the intercession of our Blessed Mother Mary and Saint Alphonsus Liguori.

The ideas included in Phase III are challenging because of the number of members needed for them to run smoothly, the amount of funding some require, and the parish support needed to carry out the activities.

However, when successful, these activities can produce great results and substantial positive attention on vocations.

During this phase, a ministry is likely focused on activities such as parish-wide events that put vocations in the forefront of all youth and their families and extend the ministry's affirmation efforts to include local seminarians. It also will hold events for altar servers and for those seriously discerning a vocation to the priesthood or religious life.

The roles continue to increase in complexity with the activities themselves, but by this time the ministry should have a group of very dedicated, experienced volunteers who can handle difficult assignments.

Possible Ministry Positions in Phase III

- See positions from Phases I and II.
- **Traveling Vocations Chalice (or Cross) Program Coordinator:** Organizes the movement of the chalice among families during Masses.
- **Let the Children Come to Me Coordinator:** Organizes adoration activities for young children.
- **Seminarian Liaison:** Updates the ministry on the progress of parish seminarians, as well as activities at the local seminary; leads efforts such as the Spiritual Adoption Program and Seminarian Care Packages.
- **Serran Liaison:** Reports on and promotes activities between the Vocation Ministry and the Serra Club (optional).

Phase IV: Expanding the Ministry's Reach

By Phase IV the Vocation Ministry is at the pinnacle of influence, operational capabilities, and visible results within the parish.

The ministry members may be asked by a young person for advice about discernment; individuals may spend more time thinking about the meaning of marriage in their spiritual lives; more young people may be seriously considering the priesthood or religious life. These and other affirming results indicate the Vocation Ministry is meeting its goals.

While the programs in Phase IV are ambitious, they are meant to develop a truly vocation-minded parish. These activities will surely bear much fruit in Jesus' name.

At this phase, the ministry should remember to share regularly the good news about successes within the ministry and the parish at large to keep people on fire for vocations.

During Phase IV, a ministry has the capacity to expand its reach beyond its own walls and is likely focused on such activities with long-term commitments from the parish, offering its service to the Office of Vocations and the nearby Serra Club, and affirming active and retired priests and religious.

Possible Ministry Positions in Phase IV

- See positions from Phases I, II, and III.
- **Youth Minister:** Reports on and promotes activities between the Vocation Ministry and youth ministry; coordinates activities within the youth ministry that promote, support, and teach about religious vocations.
- **Knights of Columbus Liaison:** Reports on and promotes activities between the Vocation Ministry and Knights of Columbus.
- **Youth Representative:** Provides the ministry with ideas for the youth.
- **Ordination Coordinator:** Coordinates reception for a newly ordained priest.
- **Discernment Coordinator:** Communicates archdiocesan discernment meetings and parish discernment retreats, dinners, and meetings to the Vocation Ministry.
- **Faith Formation Liaison:** Coordinates and facilitates promotion of vocations through various faith formation programs (adult, family, and children).
- **Ministries Liaison:** Communicates with all other ministries in the parish regarding vocations promotion, support, and education, such as young adult groups, Legion of Mary, and the like.
- **Diaconate Liaison:** Advises the ministry on diaconate activities; leads ministry meetings in prayer and reflection when a priest is not

present; provides updates on current diaconate candidate progress (optional).

- **Website Coordinator:** Responsible for keeping the ministry's website up-to-date with ministry activities (optional).

The expectation is that each Vocation Ministry will start small and simple with room to grow in size and depth. Each ministry must prayerfully and logically assess its ability to tackle a particular event. Whether a ministry is just beginning or in the process of re-energizing or expanding, deliberately growing through the four phases will lay a solid foundation on which the ministry can grow for years, helping it to build a reputation for being prudent and successful.

Also, to have a well-rounded ministry, activities should come from each of the four categories: Prayer, Awareness and Education, Youth, and Affirmation. Each category will be described in full, and will relate the types of activities, the target audiences, and the nuances that make each category important to the overall work of the ministry.

Selecting varied activities will keep the ministry members and parishioners excited and engaged. Conversely, executing a number of similar or complex activities can be draining and stressful. Consider keeping a simple diary of activities to help remind the ministry of what has been done in the past so as to avoid these pitfalls.

The implementation of each activity will be described in detail in Part II. Moreover, the Vocation Ministries Activities poster included with this book provides an easy way to compare activities to help determine which ones make the most sense.

The Power of Prayer: The Mothers of Lu, Italy

We cannot underestimate the power of prayer. In Lu, Italy, a group of Catholic mothers were lamenting the lack of priests and religious in their small Italian village. "The deepest desire of many of these mothers was for one of their sons to become a priest or for a daughter to place her life completely in God's service. Under the direction of their parish priest, Msgr. Alessandro Canora, they gathered every Tuesday for adoration of the Blessed Sacrament, asking the Lord for vocations; they also prayed for vocations after Mass."[9]

In about 60 years, over one-third of Lu's population became priests or nuns. There were 323 religious who came from the town's less than 1,000 inhabitants between 1881 and the 1940s. Through the powerful prayer of these mothers, an atmosphere of delight and Christian devotion developed in the families that helped the children to recognize their vocations more readily.

Like the mothers in Lu, our ministry knew early on that weekly or monthly adoration for vocations would be instrumental in our efforts to bringing about a vocation-minded parish and for increasing vocations overall. Jesus is waiting to be asked, and he is truly present in the Eucharist! Encourage parishioners to run to Jesus in the Blessed Sacrament and to beg for more workers in his harvest.

---

9 "The Example of Praying Mothers of Lu." www.Credidimus.wordpress.com. N.p., 10 May 2010. Web. 10 Jan. 2014.

PART
II

CHAPTER FOUR

PRAYER ACTIVITIES

The Christian life should be rooted in prayer; thus, prayer is also the foundation for a faithful Vocation Ministry. If the members allow God the Father, Jesus the Son, and the Holy Spirit to lead every aspect of the ministry, then the fruits of the labor will be great. Organizing prayer for vocations is a basic activity that any ministry can carry out. Every activity should be covered in prayer. Pray that God's holy will be done through the ministry. Pray that all who play a part in the activities—members, volunteers, and participants—will have an open heart to God's call in their lives. Through consecration, intercession, and daily prayer, the Vocation Ministry will be exactly what God wants it to be.

PHASE I

ACTIVITY 1

Consecration

As a new Vocation Ministry, our first mission was clear: Pray! Before we could minister to our parish, we first consecrated our ministry to Jesus through our Blessed Mother, the model and mother of all vocations. We consecrate our ministry at the beginning of each meeting, placing our works under our Blessed Mother's patronage each month.

Even if your ministry is not new, consider asking the Blessed Virgin Mary to intercede on behalf of the ministry and its activities to ensure they are covered in prayer.

Prayer of Consecration for a Vocation Ministry

Loving God, we praise and thank you for sending your Son among us born of the Virgin Mary. We praise you, Jesus, for founding the Church and calling us to participate in your divine life. Help all of us, in the ministry of vocations, to help you call workers to your vineyard, workers to your Church who will help you to carry on your work of redemption. We recognize the need you have for apostles in our world; priests who will bring people the fruits of the redemption which you won for us on the cross. We recognize the need for sisters and brothers to bear witness to the love of Jesus in our world and to the fact that this world is passing. We desire, Lord God, to place this our Vocation Ministry under the patronage of the one whose "Yes" has allowed you to take flesh and become our savior and brother. Mary, Mother of the Church, pray with us just as you did with the disciples in the upper room on the day of Pentecost. Help us to be open like you were to the gifts of the Holy Spirit. We consecrate our work to you so that just as you raised Jesus Christ on earth and watched him grow to maturity, now through your intercession, let us help you raise up the body of Christ on earth in the Church, by helping God's call reach the ears of our brothers and sisters in our community.

~Father Victor Perez

Overview

Goal: To consecrate the ministry to Jesus through our Blessed Mother Mary

Time of Year: Year-round, at the formation of the Vocation Ministry and each meeting thereafter

Target Audience: Vocation Ministry members

Lead Time: 1 week

Implementation: Easy

People

External Leaders: None

VM Leaders: Priest, director

Additional Volunteers: Ministry members

Resources

Materials Needed: Consecration prayer (card optional)

Funds Needed: None

Number Expected: Ministry members

Promotion: N/A

Resources Available: Consecration prayer can be downloaded from www.vocationministry.com

Instructions

1. Download the prayer.
2. Provide a copy for each Vocation Ministry member, or place the consecration prayer on the agenda for every meeting.
3. Say the prayer at the beginning of each meeting.

Notes:

—During each meeting, placing a small statue of the Blessed Mother in the middle of the group will remind the members to continue to ask for her intercession on their behalf.

ACTIVITY 2

Intercession

A long with asking for God's help and Our Blessed Mother's prayers, ask for the intercession of the saints who strived for holiness on earth and are now in heaven praying for our ministry and its activities.

While many saints can be called upon for prayers for vocations, a few, in particular, are well-known intercessors for these activities.

> **Saint Alphonsus Liguori,** Patron of Vocations and Theologians
> **Saint Junípero Serra,** Patron of Vocations
> **Saint John Vianney,** Patron of Priests
> **Saint Charles Borromeo,** Patron of Seminarians
> **St. Gabriel of Our Lady of Sorrows,** Patron of Clergy
> **Saint Monica,** Patron of Married Women
> **St. Scholastica,** Patron of Nuns

Overview

Goal: To cover daily in prayer all ministry members and their activities, as well as those for whom the ministry works, requesting intercession from the saints
Time of Year: Any
Target Audience: Vocation Ministry members
Lead Time: None
Implementation: Easy

People

External Leaders: None
VM Leaders: Director, communications coordinator
Additional Volunteers: Ministry members

Resources

Materials Needed: None
Funds Needed: None
Number Expected: Number in ministry
Promotion: N/A
Resources Available: None

Instructions

1. Ask the appropriate saint to intercede on all communications within the ministry and when communicating with other groups or organizations within the parish or diocese at-large (e.g., emails, thank-you notes, ministry meetings).

2. Place an intercessory prayer request in bulletin blurbs and other appropriate places (e.g., St. Alphonsus Liguori, pray for us. St. John Vianney, pray for our priests).

ACTIVITY 3

Prayer Drive

Prayer is powerful, and our priests are in need of prayer to sustain them in their work of salvation. Encouraging parishioners to pray for vocations, especially before the Blessed Sacrament, brings awareness to the idea of praying for our shepherds. Specifically, a prayer drive gives parishioners an opportunity to pray for priests of the parish, and it lifts and bolsters the priest who is the beneficiary of the prayers. If only one parishioner signs up to pray, which will not likely be the case, the mission is accomplished, as one extra prayer may be just what that priest needs.

Overview

Goal: To increase prayer for vocations by signing up parishioners to pray for priestly and religious vocations at a specific time and place

Time of Year: Any, especially Priesthood Sunday and World Day of Prayer for Vocations

Target Audience: Parishioners

Lead Time: 1 month

Implementation: Easy

People

External Leaders: None

VM Leaders: Priest, director, communications coordinator, affirmation coordinator

Additional Volunteers: 1-4 adults to staff sign-up table

Resources

Materials Needed: Promotional flyer, pens, prayer cards or sign-up sheet, 8½ x 11" plastic paper holder, wrapped box to receive cards

Funds Needed: $25 for copies of flyer and paper holder

Number Expected: As many as the entire parish

Promotion: Begin publicizing through bulletin, newsletter, website, and Mass announcements at least two weeks prior to the event

Resources Available: A prayer drive sign-up sheet, prayer commitment cards, promotional fliers in English and Spanish, and a banners are available at www.vocationministry.com

Instructions

1. Consult the priest/pastor for input on implementation and for his blessing.
2. Determine which ministry member will coordinate the activity.
3. Decide whether to ask parishioners to commit to pray with a sign-up sheet or on a prayer card.
4. Decide if the sign-up table should be staffed before and after each Mass.
5. If staffed, identify one or two ministry members to help. If the ministry is small, ask the youth minister, Boy Scout leader, or Knights of Columbus coordinator for volunteers.
6. Ask the liturgy director (or whomever authorizes when and where items may be displayed in the church) where the sign-up sheets or prayer cards can be placed the day of the event (such as in the narthex), and when everything should be removed.
7. Download or create promotional fliers, placing them around the parish in approved locations.
8. Download or create a sign-up sheet (including space for name, place of prayer, and time of prayer) and make several copies, or download or create prayer commitment cards and make enough copies for about 10-15% of parishioners at the parish.
9. Place a blurb in the bulletin, in Mass announcements, and any other avenues of publicity beginning at least two weeks prior to event.

10. If using prayer commitment cards, wrap a box in elegant paper with a hole at the top in which parishioners place their prayer commitment cards.

11. During sign-ups, ask parishioners to commit to pray for the parish priest(s) at a dedicated time and place.

12. Take all the prayer commitment cards or sign-up sheets and give them to the priests, in a card or small basket or box, depending on how many are received.

13. In the bulletin, thank all those who participated, adding a picture or two to share the special event with the parish at large.

Notes:

—This activity is simple to put into action and can be used to pray for any person in a religious vocation (priests, seminarians, deacons, religious, and consecrated) or for vocations in general.

PHASE II

ACTIVITY 4

Eucharistic Adoration for Vocations

A wise bishop once asked Mother Teresa how it was that she had so many vocations in her order at a time when most orders were losing many sisters.

She replied, "We were just like other religious congregations with few vocations. Then, we made a decision to have a holy hour in all our convents.... We had so many vocations in the intimacy with the Lord present in the Eucharist." When Mother Teresa died there were around 4,000 sisters in her order.[10]

Jesus is waiting to be asked, and he is truly present in the Eucharist. What makes more sense than to invite his people to enter into his heart to beg for workers for his fields? Encourage parishioners to storm the heavens with the request for more religious vocations with the confidence that no prayer goes unanswered.

Overview

Goal: To increase prayer for vocations by providing a specific time and location for such prayers
Time of Year: Weekly or monthly, year-round
Target Audience: Parishioners
Lead Time: 2 months
Implementation: Moderate

People

External Leaders: Parish adoration coordinator
VM Leaders: Priest, director, adoration for vocations coordinator, communications coordinator
Additional Volunteers: 1-2 adults to set up podium and stock materials

---

10 http://www.catholicadoration.com/ca/index.php?view=article&catid=41%3Aorganiza-tion-information&id=125%3Aadoration-and-vocations&format=pdf&option=com_content

Resources

Materials Needed: Table on which to place prayer materials (optional); inspirational reading material (optional)

Funds Needed: Varies, depending on optional materials

Number Expected: As many as the entire parish

Promotion: Begin publicizing through bulletin, website, and Mass announcements at least one month prior to event

Resources Available: Downloadable inspirational reading material and links to vendors of prayer cards and brochures at www.vocationministry.com

Instructions

1. Consult the priest/pastor before moving forward for input on frequency and implementation and for his blessing.
2. Determine who will coordinate the activity.
3. Firm up details, such as day(s), frequency, and table for prayer material.
4. Download, order, or find inspirational reading material that will be available each 24-hour period that highlights vocations, such as scripture readings, litanies, and prayers. This can also include prayer cards, brochures and the like.
5. Begin publicizing through bulletin, website, and Mass announcements at least one month prior to the event.

Notes:

—It may be tempting to rotate the days this event takes place every week or month so that regular adorers on each adoration opportunity have may pray for vocations in front of the Blessed Sacrament. However, it can be difficult to promote and keep track of that date each month. Using a fixed day of the week or month may be easier, but feel free to experiment until finding the day that best suits the schedules of the parish and its parishioners.

—On the day of Adoration for Vocations, consider placing a sign outside the adoration chapel asking parishioners to pray for vocations during their time with the Blessed Sacrament.

—A pamphlet or short booklet (two to three pages) can be helpful to guide parishioners in their time before the Blessed Sacrament.

ACTIVITY 5

Prayer Cards for Vocations

Many parishioners want to pray for vocations but do not always remember to do so. A ministry can help by handing out prayer cards at different times, which allows the ministry to interact with parishioners, encouraging them to pray for vocations.

Whether the prayer cards are used year-round after each daily Mass or for personal devotion given in conjunction with a special vocation day like World Day for Consecrated Life, each prayer is important.

Prayer cards can also be given out for married couples on Saint Valentine's Day.

The main idea of any vocation prayer is to pray that the individual heart remains open to God's will, especially for those who have not replied to his invitation.

Overview

Goal: To increase prayer for vocations by distributing prayer cards to parishioners

Time of Year: Year-round, especially in conjunction with a special vocation day such as World Day for Consecrated Life, Priesthood Sunday, National Vocation Awareness Week, and World Priest Day

Target Audience: Parishioners

Lead Time: 4-6 weeks

Implementation: Easy

People

External Leaders: None

VM Leaders: Priest, director, activity coordinator, communications coordinator

Additional Volunteers: 2+ adults, teens from youth ministry, or Knights of Columbus to hand out prayer cards after each Mass

Resources

Materials Needed: Printed prayer cards

Funds Needed: About 5-10 cents per card

Number Needed: Varies, depending on size of parish and if used on special days, weekend Masses, and/or daily Mass

Promotion: N/A

Resources Available: A variety of prayer cards and links to prayer card vendors are available at www.vocationministry.com

Instructions

1. Consult the priest/pastor before moving forward for input on implementation and his blessing.
2. Determine who will coordinate the activity.
3. Taking into account what the pastor/priest advised, decide what kind of prayer card is needed (after daily Mass or to enhance another activity) and create or order the cards.
4. Hand out prayer cards at specific Masses for special vocation days or keep the prayer cards available year around on a table in the narthex or the adoration chapel.

Notes:

—Consider printing the prayer cards in all languages represented at the parish.

—Prayer cards can be created for other audiences as well. For example, if a priest frequently visits nursing homes and hospitals, download from www.vocationministry.com a prayer card that guides those who are suffering to offer up their pains and sorrows to Jesus' Sacred Heart for an increase of vocations.

ACTIVITY 6

Spiritual Bouquets

The gift of prayer is a beautiful way for children and adults to show appreciation for their priest. A Spiritual Bouquet is the offering of a Holy Rosary, Mass, an hour of Eucharistic Adoration, a Chaplet of Divine Mercy, or other personal prayers for another person. These gifts of prayer are given to priests to lift them up on their special days like Priesthood Sunday, Easter, Christmas, their birthdays or ordination anniversaries.

These gifts of affirmation also balance the more challenging aspects of priestly ministry, and let him know how much parishioners pray for and appreciate his daily sacrifices.

Overview

Goal: To encourage and show appreciation for parish priest(s) by offering prayers from parishioners

Time of Year: Year-round, especially before Priesthood Sunday, Easter, Christmas, and priest's birthday and ordination anniversary

Target Audience: Parishioners

Lead Time: 1 month

Implementation: Easy

People

External Leaders: None

VM Leaders: Priest, Vocation Ministry director, affirmation coordinator, Spanish-speaking representative, communications coordinator

Additional Volunteers: 1 adult to keep materials stocked

Resources

Materials Needed: Promotional flyer, spiritual bouquet cards, pens for writing personal prayers, holder for pens and cards, basket, 8½ x 11" plastic paper holder

Funds Needed: < $100 a year

Number Expected: Roughly 10 percent of the parish participating multiple times

Promotion: Begin publicizing through bulletin, newsletter, website, and Mass announcements at least two weeks prior to event

Resources Available: Spiritual Bouquet cards in black and white and in color, and a promotional flyer can be found at www.vocationministry.com

Instructions

1. Consult the priest/pastor before moving forward for input on frequency and implementation, and for his blessing.
2. Determine who will coordinate the activity.
3. Decide if this activity should be offered year-round in the adoration chapel or as a one-time event for a special day such as Priesthood Sunday or the priest's birthday.
4. Ask the liturgy director (or whomever authorizes displaying items in the church and/or adoration chapel) if the spiritual bouquet cards may be placed in the narthex or chapel, when they may be placed, when they should be removed, and where and when promotional fliers may be placed.
5. Download or create spiritual bouquets, including the following sections.
   - From (for name of parishioner)
   - To (for name of priest)
   - Type of prayer gift (Rosary, Mass, an hour of Eucharistic Adoration, a Chaplet of Divine Mercy, or other)
   - Note (for a short note of appreciation)
6. Download or create promotional flyer.
7. Provide a basket or container in which parishioners may drop completed cards.
8. Repeatedly announce the activity in the bulletin, at Mass, and through other appropriate avenues, especially before special occasions.
9. Keep the cards and pens stocked in a permanent location if possible, such as in the adoration chapel or in the foyer.
10. Present the priest with the collection of cards prior to special holidays or occasions.
11. In the bulletin, thank all those who participated.

Notes:

—This affirming activity can be adapted for parish deacons, seminarians, and consecrated brothers or sisters.

—If the Spiritual Bouquets are offered year-round, consider changing the promotional flyer every few months, or for new occasions to bring

attention to the activity for those who are used to seeing the display
and bouquets all the time.

ACTIVITY 7

World Day Of Prayer for Vocations (Parish)

In 1964 Pope Paul VI designated that World Day of Prayer for Vocations would be celebrated on Good Shepherd Sunday. This is the day each year that all Catholics are asked to pray to God that he send more workers into the harvest. At the parish level, this is a perfect opportunity to bring together all parishioners to pray for vocations to the priesthood and religious life, especially before the Blessed Sacrament.

This event can take many forms, such as a day of adoration for vocations in the chapel or a Holy Hour in the church with a reception afterwards. Even if the parish does not have an event, it is good to encourage parishioners to pray for vocations on these days.

Overview

Goal: To offer parishioners an opportunity to pray for vocations, especially to the priesthood and the consecrated religious life

Time of Year: World Day of Prayer for Vocations (Good Shepherd Sunday)

Target Audience: Parishioners

Lead Time: 3 months

Implementation: Moderate

People

External Leaders: None

VM Leaders: Priest, director, activity coordinator, special events coordinator, communications coordinator

Additional Volunteers: 2-12 adults and/or youth ministry for reception set-up and cleanup

Resources

Materials Needed: Program for Holy Hour (see Reception on page 189)

Funds Needed: $200 plus, depending on reception and rosary rings or another gift that can be given to parishioners after Masses or at the reception

Number Expected: All parishioners

Promotion: Begin publicizing through bulletin, newsletter, website, and Mass announcements at least one month prior to event

Resources Available: A sample program and two different banners are available at www.vocationministry.com

Instructions

1. Consult the priest/pastor for input on implementation and for his blessing.
2. Determine who will coordinate the activity.
3. Determine the extent of the activity (Holy Hour, reception, rosary rings or other gifts).
4. Plan the program (readings, music).
5. Plan the reception (see activity on page 189).
6. Order rosary rings.
7. Publicize the event through the bulletin, newsletter, website, and Mass announcements at least two months in advance.
8. Create a simple program for the event.
9. Set up for, enjoy, and clean up after the reception.
10. In the bulletin, thank all those who participated, adding a picture or two to share the special event with the parish at large.

PHASE III

ACTIVITY 8

Let the Children Come to Me

J esus said, "Let the children come to me" (Matthew 19:14). Children's hearts are so open to hearing God's call. Let us give them every opportunity to talk to God about his plan for their lives. We may not know all the fruits that come when we teach the youngest parishioners to adore before the Blessed Sacrament, but rest assured that seeds of holiness are planted.

Overview

Goal: To teach children to pray for God's will in their lives before the Blessed Sacrament
Time of Year: Any
Target Audience: Children of the parish, especially pre-kindergarteners through fourth graders (ages 4-10)
Lead Time: 3 months
Implementation: Moderate

People

External Leaders: School principal and/or religious education director, parish facilities coordinator
VM Leaders: Priest, director, Let the Children Come to Me coordinator, special events coordinator, school liaison, faith formation liaison, communications coordinator
Additional Volunteers: 2-12 adults and/or youth ministry for reception set-up and cleanup

Resources

Materials Needed: Simple program for event; see Receptions on page 189
Funds Needed: Varies, depending on reception
Number Expected: Up to all families in the parish

Promotion: Begin publicizing through bulletin, newsletter, website, fliers, and Mass announcements at least one month prior to event

Resources Available: A banner/flier can be found at www.vocationministry.com

Instructions

1. Consult the priest/pastor before moving forward for input on implementation and for his blessing. Ask if he or another priest or deacon will expose the Blessed Sacrament and lead the children in adoration.

2. Determine the date of the event. If the parish offers religious education classes on a weeknight, consider offering the event after the last meeting of the year or the week after the previous meeting. The parents and children will be used to coming to the parish grounds at this day and time, which bolsters attendance.

3. Determine who will coordinate the activity.

4. Coordinate a place for the reception with the parish facilities coordinator.

5. Plan the ceremony to include scripture reading(s), songs, and a short talk by the priest. Include songs that children know and love, such as *O Come Let us Adore Him* and *Jesus Loves Me*, to increase their involvement and enjoyment. Limit the ceremony to 30-40 minutes to keep the children's attention.

6. Plan the reception (see activity on page 189). The simplest reception can be outside on the parish grounds so that the parents can mingle and children can run around and play after they eat.

7. Create a simple program for the ceremony that includes the scripture and song lyrics.

8. Begin publicizing through bulletin, newsletter, website, fliers to religious education classes, and Mass announcements at least a month in advance of event.

9. Set up for, enjoy, and clean up after the reception.

10. In the bulletin, thank all those who participated, adding a picture or two to share the special event with the parish at large.

11. Send a thank you note to each external leader, expressing the ministry's gratitude for their help in the success of the activity.

Notes:

—If the event takes place in early May, consider adding a May Crowning event after adoration, where the children bring flowers and crown a statue of our Blessed Mother in the church courtyard.

—Considering holding the program during religious education class time, which would minimize efforts and maximize attendance.

ACTIVITY 9

Traveling Vocations Chalice Program

The Traveling Vocations Chalice Program was created and is promoted by the Serra Club. The main idea is that a chalice used in the sacrifice of the Mass is sent home with families within the parish. Not only is this a symbol of the priesthood you want to imprint in the minds of all those who see it, but it also promotes the Eucharist. Having the chalice at home for a week is a reminder for individuals and the parents and children in a family to pray for and think about their own vocation. This program has the potential to bring about a vocation-minded parish, one family at a time.

Overview

Goal: To raise awareness of vocations and to remind children, individuals, and families to pray about their vocation and vocations, in general, by sending a chalice to their homes for a short time as a reminder

Time of Year: Any, but it's great to kick off during National Vocation Awareness Week or World Day of Prayer for Vocations

Target Audience: All families and individuals in the parish, especially students in parish school and/or religious education classes

Lead Time: 6 months+

Implementation: Complex

People

External Leaders: School principal and/or the religious education director

VM Leaders: Priest, director, Traveling Vocations Chalice Program coordinator, school liaison, faith formation liaison, communications coordinator

Additional Volunteers: 1-4 adults to help coordinate the travel of the chalice

Resources

Materials Needed: 1-4 chalices and cases, depending on size of parish and approach; flyer; 1-4 binders of prayer material

Funds Needed: $100-$1,000, depending on number of chalices traveling and donated materials

Number Expected: As many as all families and individuals in parish

Promotion: Begin publicizing through bulletin, newsletter, website, and Mass announcements at least one month prior to event

Resources Available: Find prayer, information, binder material, chalice, and case sources at www.vocationministry.com

Instructions

1. Consult the priest/pastor before moving forward, for input on implementation and for his blessing.
2. Determine who will coordinate the activity.
3. Determine the target audience: students in parish school, children in religious education classes, and/or families and individuals at weekend Masses.
4. Consult with the appropriate leader (principal or religious education director) for permission and to determine the best time for the activity.
5. Determine as a ministry—based on the pastor's recommendation, size of your parish, and budget—how many chalices and carrying cases to use.
6. Ask the Knights of Columbus liaison if the parish council would be willing either to donate money to the effort or to donate a chalice and/or a case.
7. Determine how to obtain materials not donated. Be flexible, asking other parish ministries for help. Normally, donors to the project have their names engraved on a plaque on the back of the chalice case. The Knights of Columbus may choose to have their

symbol and council number placed at the base of the chalice. One parishioner may donate wood for the case and another may be willing to construct it.

8. Download and print the prayer materials, information, and instructions that will travel with the chalice(s), customizing the cover page of the binder to reflect the target audience.

9. Ask the pastor to write a letter to the families and individuals who will receive the chalice, explaining the importance of prayers for vocations by parishioners.

10. Find other appropriate materials that may travel with the case, such as a Fishers of Men DVD or prayer cards for the family to keep.

11. Coordinate for the chalice to move from class to class (school, religion classes, and/or parish religious education classes), staying at each class for up to a week. It is best for the principal or religious education director to coordinate the movement of the chalice while it is in his or her possession.

12. Have the chalice(s) and case(s) blessed, preferably in front of the students or children. For example, if the case will start traveling in the parish school's religion classes first, have it blessed at a schoolwide Mass.

13. When the chalice is in the classroom, ask the principal to oversee that the teachers ask children to pray the age-appropriate prayers for vocations.

14. Communicate to parish families through fliers, the bulletin, newsletters, the website, and Mass announcements the opportunity to sign up to take the chalice home after weekend Mass and return it to the parish office by noon the following Friday, or back to the Mass from which they received the case.

15. Conduct sign-ups through email, phone calls, and/or a sign-up table at Mass. Depending on the process, families may choose the week they have the chalice during sign-ups, or a volunteer may call each family to coordinate the schedule.

16. Arrange to have the chalice on display, maybe on a small pedestal, for the blessing and exchange during Mass.

17. Contact the family the week before their scheduled week to ensure they will attend Mass.

18. Meet the family prior to Mass to give them instructions on receiving their blessing and the chalice during Mass. Give them the prayer binder of instructions to take home.

19. The family receives the chalice and case during Mass.

20. Email the family later that week to remind them to return the chalice, case, and binder to the parish office by noon on Friday or to that same Mass.

21. If necessary, clean the chalice and case, and reprint binder information and instructions.

22. Send a thank you note to each external leader, expressing the ministry's gratitude for their help in the success of the activity.

Notes:

—Larger parishes may choose to use more than one chalice to expedite the program, or they may prefer the impact of having each participating family receive the same chalice.

—If feasible, sign-ups can be conducted on the parish website.

—Consider asking the Youth Minister, a group of home school children, or an American Heritage Girl troop if they would like to make rosaries to include with the chalice as gifts for each family.

—The children's awareness of the chalice from seeing it at school or religious education spurs families' involvement, as does beginning sign-ups during the first week the chalice is in the schools when it is fresh in the children's minds.

—Include a photo of the chalice in all written or electronic communication to increase awareness and recognition.

—During the summer or times when the chalice is not traveling through the school or Masses, consider asking groups like the Knights of Columbus to promote the chalice within their organization.

—After researching other successful Traveling Vocations Chalice Programs, most parishes ask staff members to help with the weekly details.

ACTIVITY 10

Traveling Vocations Cross Program

This activity, similar to the Traveling Vocations Chalice Program, asks for prayers for vocations as parishioners take home a standing crucifix or cross with an Agnus Dei, a figure of a lamb bearing a cross. It is perfect for traveling through parish schools, religious education classes, or Masses. Newer ministries may want to start with the Traveling Vocations Cross Program, as it is more cost effective and potentially less labor-intensive. It was created and is promoted by Serra.

Overview

Goal: To raise awareness of vocations and to remind children, individuals, and families to pray about their vocation and vocations in general by having a cross in their classroom or by sending a cross to their homes for a short time as a reminder

Time of Year: Any, especially great to kick off during National Vocation Awareness Week or World Day of Prayer for Vocations

Target Audience: Students in parish school and/or in religious education classes, families, and individuals at weekend Masses

Lead Time: 3+ months

Implementation: Moderate

People

External Leaders: School principal and/or religious education director

VM Leaders: Priest, director, Traveling Vocations Cross (or Chalice) Program coordinator, school liaison, faith formation liaison, communications coordinator

Additional Volunteers: 2 or more adults to help coordinate the travel of the cross, depending on if it travels through the Sunday Masses or not

Resources

Materials Needed: 1-4 standing crosses, depending on size of parish and approach; flyer; 1-4 prayer binders

Funds Needed: $20+, depending on the type of cross purchased

Number Expected: As many as all families and individuals in parish, and the number of children at parish school and/or in religious education classes

Promotion: If traveling the Masses, begin publicizing through bulletin, newsletter, website, and Mass announcements at least one month prior to event

Resources Available: Prayer, information, and binder material at www.vocationministry.com

Instructions

1. Consult the priest/pastor before moving forward for input on implementation and for his blessing.
2. Determine who will coordinate the activity.
3. Determine the target audience: students in parish school, children in religious education classes, and/or at Masses.
4. Determine as a ministry, based on the pastor's recommendation, size of your parish, and budget, how many crosses to use.
5. If the cross is to travel to the parish school's religion classes, consult with the appropriate leader (principal or religious education director) for permission and to determine the best time for the activity.
6. Obtain a standing cross, either a crucifix or with Agnus Dei attached. Let it be known that the ministry is in need of one, and it may be donated.
7. Have the cross blessed, preferably in front of the target audience. For example, if the cross will start traveling in the parish religious education classes first, have it blessed at a Mass that many children from that program attend.
8. Download and print prayer material, information, and instructions, and create a binder that will travel with each cross, customizing the cover page of the binder to reflect the target audience.
9. Ask the pastor to write a letter to the families and individuals who will receive the cross, explaining the importance of parishioners praying for vocations.
10. Coordinate for the cross to move from class to class (school religion classes and/or parish religious education classes), staying at each class for up to a week. It is best to have the principal or

director of Religious Education to coordinate the movement of the cross while it is in his or her possession.

11. When the cross is in the classrooms, ask the principal to oversee that the teachers ask children to pray the age-appropriate prayers for vocations.

12. Simultaneously, communicate to parish families through fliers, the bulletin, newsletters, the website, and Mass announcements the opportunity to sign up to take the cross home after weekend Mass and return it to the parish office by noon the following Friday or back to the Mass from which they received the case.

13. Conduct sign-ups through email, phone calls, and/or a sign-up table at Mass. Depending on the process, families may choose the week they have the cross during sign-ups, or a volunteer may call each family to coordinate the schedule.

14. Arrange to have the cross on display, maybe on a small pedestal, for the blessing and exchange during Mass.

15. Contact the family the week before their scheduled week to ensure they will attend Mass.

16. Meet the family prior to Mass to give them instructions on receiving their blessing and the cross during Mass, and the prayer binder of instructions to take home.

17. The family receives the cross and case during Mass.

18. Email the family later that week to remind them to return the cross to the parish office by noon on Friday or to that same Mass.

19. If necessary, clean the cross and reprint binder information and instructions.

20. Send a thank you note to each external leader, expressing the ministry's gratitude for their help in the success of the activity.

21. In the bulletin, thank the religious classes for participating and at the same time, educate the parishioners, adding a picture or two to share this special event with the parish at large.

Notes:

—Larger parishes may choose to use more than one cross to expedite the program, or they may prefer the impact of having each participating family receive the same cross.

—If feasible, sign-ups can be conducted on the parish website.

—The children's awareness of the cross from seeing it at school or religious education spurs families' involvement, as does beginning sign-ups during the first week the cross is in the schools when it is fresh in the children's minds.

—Include a photo of the cross in all written or electronic communication to increase awareness and recognition.

—During the summer or times when the cross is not traveling through the school or Masses, consider asking groups like the Knights of Columbus to promote the cross within their organization.

—Consider asking staff members to help with the weekly details.

PHASE IV

ACTIVITY 11

Family Holy Hour for Vocations

"In the Eucharist, the Son of God comes to meet us and desires to become one with us; Eucharistic Adoration is simply the natural consequence of the Eucharistic Celebration, which is itself the Church's supreme act of adoration." [11]

Every effort should be made to bring parishioners before the Lord in the Blessed Sacrament to pray for their vocation and vocations in general, but especially on World Day of Prayer for Vocations. This activity encourages families to attend, so parents model praying to their children.

The beauty is in the simplicity of prayer for vocations as the focus is on Jesus Christ in the Blessed Sacrament at the Family Holy Hour for Vocations.

Overview

Goal: To increase prayer for vocations by providing a specific hour on this special day for families to pray for vocations together

Time of Year: World Day of Prayer for Vocations (Good Shepherd Sunday)

Target Audience: Parish families

Lead Time: 2 months

Implementation: Moderate

People

External Leaders: None

VM Leaders: Priest, director, adoration for vocations coordinator, special events coordinator, communications coordinator

Additional Volunteers: 2-12 adults and/or youth ministry for reception set-up and cleanup

---

11 Pope Benedict XVI. "Post-synodal Apostolic Exhortation Sacramentum Caritatis." www.vatican.va. N.p., 2007. Web. 28 Dec. 2013.

Resources

Materials Needed: Program or worship aid for event (see Reception on page 189)

Funds Needed: $100-$500, depending on reception

Number Expected: As many as all parishioners

Promotion: Inclusion in the bulletin and weekend Mass announcements at least one month in advance, place fliers around campuses, send bulletin blurb and announcement to surrounding parishes, advertise on local Catholic radio for free, place a blurb in the classified section of the diocesan newspaper

Resources Available: A program and inspirational prayer material at www.vocationministry.com

Instructions

1. Consult the priest/pastor for input on implementation (e.g., songs, scripture readings, and litany) and for his blessing.
2. Determine who will coordinate the activity.
3. Determine the scope of the event (adoration, reception, gift for attendees, such as prayer cards).
4. Coordinate a place for the reception with the parish facilities coordinator.
5. Plan adoration to focus on Jesus in the Blessed Sacrament, which may include a litany for vocations, music, and parishioners reading scripture in English, Spanish, or possibly another language spoken widely at the parish
6. Begin publicizing through bulletin, newsletter, website, and Mass announcements at least one month prior to event.
7. Plan the Holy Hour for Vocations reception, if applicable (see activity on page 189).
8. Download or create a program for the event.
9. Download or create inspirational prayer material for the event, if desired.
10. Set up for, enjoy, and clean up after reception (if applicable).
11. In the bulletin, thank all those who participated, adding a picture or two to share this special event with the parish at large and encourage attendance in the future.

Notes:

—Conducting the Holy Hour in English and Spanish, or other prominent language spoken in the parish, is a visible way to unite the parish in prayer.

— A reception, though optional, gives all the opportunity to get to know the families, the religious, and priests.

—Consider inviting other priests, seminarians, and religious, to the event. They can witness to the joy of answering God's call.

ACTIVITY 12

Pray for Seminarian Cards

Seminarians and all those in religious formation face a roller coaster of emotions. They are often thrilled at finding and following their calling, stressed during parts of the education and discernment, and uncertain during times of doubt. Worldly influences can be a distraction. Supernatural forces would love nothing more than to bring struggle to those in formation. Prayers are vital to help these men to remain close to our Lord, especially in the Blessed Sacrament, and to our Blessed Mother.

Overview

Goal: To engage parishioners in praying for seminarians by distributing prayer cards

Time of Year: Year-round, but consider special times such as World Day of Prayer for Vocations or at the beginning of the semester

Target Audience: Parishioners, seminarians

Lead Time: 1 month

Implementation: Easy

People

External Leaders: None

VM Leaders: Priest, director, seminarian liaison, communications coordinator

Additional Volunteers: 2+ adults, youth ministry, or Knights of Columbus to hand out prayer cards

Resources

Materials Needed: Printed prayer cards
Funds Needed: About 5 cents per card
Number Needed: Varies, depending on size of parish and if used on special days, weekend Masses, and/or daily Mass
Promotion: N/A
Resources Available: Sample prayer at www.vocationministry.com

Instructions

1. Consult the priest/pastor before moving forward for input on implementation and card design, and for his blessing.
2. Determine who will coordinate the activity.
3. Decide how many prayer cards are needed.
4. Create or order prayer cards.
5. Hand out prayer cards after specific Masses on special days such as World Day of Prayer for Vocations or the beginning of the school year.

Notes:

—Sample daily prayer for seminarians:

Loving God, I ask for a special blessing and outpouring of the Holy Spirit on (seminarian's name), whom you have called to the seminary. Let his vocation grow and develop through a deep spirit of prayer and by following the path of Jesus Christ your Son. May Mary protect him from all harm and through her powerful intercession obtain for him all the graces he needs to grow into the image of Jesus, the high priest. Give him the grace to embrace the cross through all difficulties, knowing that faith is made strong through trials. Make the yoke easy and the burden light by keeping him ever close to the loving Heart of your Son. Amen.

Fr. Victor Perez

—Consider printing the prayer cards in all languages represented at the parish.

—This activity can be easily adapted for men and women in religious formation.

ACTIVITY 13

Spiritual Adoption Program

While seminarians are thankful for the desire to intimately serve Christ and his Church, the journey to ordination can be filled with struggles, uncertainty, and hesitation. With the help of the Holy Spirit, the Blessed Mother's powerful intercession, and the affirmation and prayers of a dedicated family or individual, the discerner can receive the grace needed to continue his journey.

Overview

Goal: For a family or individual to adopt a seminarian, promising to affirm him and pray daily for him for an extended period

Time of Year: Year-round for one or more years

Target Audience: Parishioners, seminarians (either from parish or diocese or from local seminary)

Lead Time: 3-6 months

Implementation: Complex

People

External Leaders: Seminary rector or staff member

VM Leaders: Priest, director, seminarian liaison, communications coordinator

Additional Volunteers: Adults to recruit families and individuals to pray for seminarians

Resources

Materials Needed: None

Funds Needed: None

Number Expected: All seminarians and enough parishioners to match with them

Promotion: If decided upon, begin publicizing through bulletin, newsletter, website, fliers, and Mass announcements at least one month prior to event

Resources Available: Sample questionnaire for seminarians at www.vocationministry.com

Instructions

1. Consult the priest/pastor before moving forward, asking for his input and blessing. Ask his preference of how many seminarians to pair with parishioners, and recommendations on finding families/partners by word of mouth or through promotion of the program.

2. Determine who will coordinate the activity.

3. Determine the date to launch the program.

4. Decide which seminarians to adopt—all seminarians, just diocesan seminarians, seminarians from other dioceses, or only those from the parish.

5. Depending on the amount of interaction expected between the affirming family/partner and seminarian, meeting with rector of seminary to discuss the program may be advisable.

6. Depending on how the pastor/ministry wants to find affirming families/partners, either explain the program to parishioners through bulletin, newsletter, website, and Mass announcements at least two months in advance, or ask ministry members to quietly invite faithful parishioners to pray for a seminarian.

7. Provide a way for families or individuals in the parish to sign up to participate.

8. Match seminarians with families or individuals.

9. Provide all participants an information sheet that explains the goal of the program:
    - Pray daily for and affirm a specific seminarian for at least one year, providing encouragement during the discernment process.
    - Remember the seminarians in daily prayer, Eucharistic Adoration, The Rosary, Novenas, and Mass intentions.

10. Send parishioners periodic emails with ideas on how to encourage their seminarians while at the same time fostering vocations in their own family:
    - Pray as a family for the seminarians in diocese.
    - Invite a priest, brother or sister to the home.
    - Attend an Ordination Mass, Holy Hour, or Prayer Vigil for Vocations with family.
    - Let children see an openness and love of God's will.
    - Find opportunities to affirm the gifts and talents of children, helping them relate their gifts to serving God.
    - Read vocation stories in scripture, such as Samuel, The Annunciation, and Jesus calling the Apostles.
11. The second year, after praying for their seminarian for a year, the ministry can expand the program, asking the parishioners to send their seminarian a special note of affirmation during holidays, birthdays, or special feast days.
12. Send a thank you note to each external leader, expressing the ministry's gratitude for their help in the success of the activity.

Notes:

—This program can be adapted to include novices in religious life.

—Often the seminarians in most need of encouragement are those from other countries.

—Matching seminarians and parishioners with deliberation, based on culture, location, or other commonalities, is ideal but not always possible.

—Hosting a reception at which the seminarian and parishioners meet provides a great end for the Year of Prayer.

—Sample Note of Affirmation:

Dear Thomas,

Welcome to the Finley family! You have been spiritually adopted! You are now a part of our daily prayer life. You can be confident we are praying every day for your protection, perseverance and peace. We are grateful and inspired by your "Yes" to God's call.

Many Blessings,

James, Isabella, Sam, Elizabeth, Mary, Will, David, Jane and John

World Day of Prayer for Vocations (Diocese)

When the ministry is running at full strength, consider contacting the Office of Vocations in your diocese to offer help with any event it is planning. Normally, the Director of Vocations is overwhelmed with vocation activities and could do even more if they had assistance from others who have hearts for vocations.

One event in particular that can have a wide effect in the diocese is World Day of Prayer for Vocations. This worthwhile activity will develop a sense of a community praying for vocations.

By coordinating with other organizations, holding a diocesan event becomes a manageable task.

No matter what the Office of Vocations needs, letting the staff know that the ministry members are willing to help and are praying for vocations will be music to their ears.

Overview

Goal: To invite parishioners to pray for vocations to the priesthood and the consecrated religious life with others in the diocese

Time of Year: World Day of Prayer for Vocations (4th Sunday of Easter, Good Shepherd Sunday)

Target Audience: Parishioners, major groups such as Knights of Columbus, Serrans, American Heritage Girls, and college students in the diocese

Lead Time: 8-12 months

Implementation: Complex

People

External Leaders: Office of Vocations director or staff, leaders of various groups, and organizations within the diocese

VM Leaders: Priest, director, activity coordinator, special events coordinator

Additional Volunteers: Ministry members to participate; 4-12 adults for planning, helping with the exhibit (if applicable), and sign-in; adults for reception set-up and cleanup

Resources

Materials Needed: Worship aid for Holy Hours; see Reception on page 189

Funds Needed: Varies, depending on reception and stipends for those leading praise and worship. If you are helping the diocese, they probably have a budget for activities like this.

Number Expected: As many as all parishioners in diocese, realistically 300-600 people, depending on size of diocese and promotion of event

Promotion: Begin publicizing the event through the bulletin, newsletter, website, and Mass announcements, and to other parishes and groups in diocese, and the diocese at large through the local Catholic newspaper at least two months in advance

Resources Available: Program, inspirational prayer material, and an optional novena for vocations at www.vocationministry.com

Instructions

1. Consult the priest/pastor for input on implementation and for his blessing, since the energies and possibly funds from the Vocation Ministry would be used outside of the parish.
2. Determine who will coordinate the activity.
3. Meet with the diocesan vocations director to gauge interest in holding a diocesan-wide World Day of Prayer for Vocations.
4. Including the diocesan vocation director, discuss ideas for this event, determining the scope of the event in terms of adoration, exhibit, and reception (see activities on pages 62, 119, 189).
5. Determine extent of the activity (worship aid, inspirational prayer material, groups to invite, special youth hour).
6. Plan the schedule for adoration. Decide whether certain groups adoring together would be the best way to foster fellowship. Here is a sample of a schedule of the day:

9:30 a.m.	Mass
10:45 a.m.	Exposition directly following Mass
11 a.m.-Noon	Serrans/Parish Vocation Committees

Noon-1 p.m.	Knights of Columbus/Sovereign Military Order Malta/Knights of Peter Claver/Catholic Daughters
1-2 p.m.	Catholic Elementary and Junior High School Students/Home School Students/Boys Scouts of America/Girl Scouts/Altar Servers/American Heritage Girls
2-3 p.m.	Priests/Deacons/Religious/St. Vincent de Paul Society/Parents of seminarians/Lay Movements of the Catholic Church
3-4 p.m.	High School Students/College Students/ Young Adults Vocation Discerners—Praise and Worship Music
4-5 p.m.	Encuentros y grupos juveniles/Movimiento Familiar/Guadalupanos/y otros Movimientos La icos de la Iglesia Católica/Jóvenes en discernimiento vocacional—Alabanza y Musica de Adoración
5-5:10 p.m.	Benediction and Reposition of the Blessed Sacrament

7. Disseminate schedule of groups who will be worshiping together to each group.
8. Plan the reception, if applicable (see activity on page 189).
9. Plan the exhibit, if applicable (see activity on page 119)
10. Invite other parishes, groups, and ministries to the event, providing details such as goal, location, and schedule.
11. Publicize the event through the local Catholic newspaper and radio, the Office of Vocations, through parish bulletin, newsletter, website, and Mass announcements at least two months in advance.
12. Gather or download booklets of scripture, songs, litanies, and prayers in English and Spanish for adorers to use for inspiration (optional).
13. Provide sign-in sheets at each entrance, gathering the attendee's name, parish, and the group he/she is representing such as Catholic Daughters of America, which can help determine who pro-

moted the event to their members and which parishes are represented. Offer name tags that help promote fellowship (optional).

14. Set up for, enjoy, and clean up after the reception.

15. Send a thank you note to each external leader, expressing the ministry's gratitude for their help in the success of the activity.

16. In the bulletin, thank all those who attended, adding a picture or two to share this special event with the parish at large.

Notes:

—In addition to praying for vocations to the priesthood and the consecrated religious life, beg the Holy Spirit to pour down a wellspring of grace on the parish that will foster vocations in families.

—Sample program:

> **Song:** Holy God We Praise Thy Name
> **Scripture:** Luke 10: 1-4—Begin immediately after the song
> **Reflection:** 2-3 minutes
> **Silent Reflection:** 2-3 minutes
> **Litany for Vocations**
> **Silent Reflection:** Until the 55-minute mark
> **Vocation Prayer:** Five minutes before hour is complete

—Consider a special Holy Hour for the youth that includes praise and worship music. Youth ministers within the archdiocese will be great sources of ideas.

—Consider a special Holy Hour in each language represented in the archdiocese or a Cultural Holy Hour where many cultures are represented. For example, Vietnamese Dominican Sisters can lead the song, a seminarian, priest, or parishioner from another country can read the scripture passage.

—Consider distributing a vocation prayer card at the event as a gift.

—Consider emailing a novena for vocations to ministry members and/or those attending, starting nine days prior to the event.

CHAPTER FIVE

AWARENESS AND EDUCATION ACTIVITIES

Pope Benedict XVI said, "Each of you has a personal vocation which He has given you for your own joy and sanctity."[12] The Vocation Ministry should bring awareness to this fact in a myriad of ways, encouraging every parishioner, adult, and child to ask God, "What is your plan for my life? What will bring me ultimate joy?"

One of the primary purposes of the Vocation Ministry is to lovingly, prayerfully, and frequently present the priesthood, religious life, and marriage as the options to be discerned and explain how that discernment process is to be completed.

12 http://www.vatican.va/holy_father/benedict_xvi/homilies/2008/documents/hf_ben-xvi_hom_20080719_cathedral_en.html

PHASE I

ACTIVITY 15

Book Rack Materials

The area in the narthex where magazines, prayer cards and pamphlets are displayed gets passed hundreds of times during the week and often thousands of times on Sunday. Placing materials here can bring vocations awareness to the parishioners in a passive and cost-effective manner.

These materials should inspire parents and youth to think about some aspect of vocations—anything from sharing how to pray a rosary for vocations or about what life is like as a religious sister.

Overview

Goal: To increase awareness of, interest in, and involvement in vocations by making vocation materials available to parishioners
Time of Year: Year-round
Target Audience: Parishioners
Lead Time: 1 month
Implementation: Easy

People

External Leaders: None
VM Leaders: Priest, director, communications coordinator
Additional Volunteers: None

Resources

Materials Needed: Magazines, pamphlets, brochures, and prayer cards
Funds Needed: Varies; some materials are free
Number Expected: Up to all parishioners
Promotion: Include blurb in bulletin, newsletter, website, and Mass announcements that materials are available
Resources Available: See a list of promotional materials at www.vocationministry.com

Instructions

1. Consult the priest/pastor for input on implementation and for his blessing.
2. Determine who will coordinate the activity.
3. Taking into account the ministry budget, decide as a ministry which resources best fit the needs of the parish.
4. Make sure the parish has a book rack; if not, obtain one with proper permission.
5. Order and stock the book rack regularly.

Notes:

—Vianney Vocations has a large selection of vocation-related, printed materials available. You can find all of their high-quality resources at www.vianneyvocations.com.

—Take note of which materials disappear most quickly. This information may guide the ministry on which type of media is most attractive to parishioners and will help with reordering or reprinting decisions.

ACTIVITY 16

Bulletin

One of the easiest ways to promote vocations is through the parish bulletin, and it is free! Advertise upcoming events, write recaps of recent events, thank everyone who attended, and share success stories. Include photos at every opportunity to attract attention. In between activities, submit pre-written blurbs that will provoke thought about vocations. When parishioners see the Vocation Ministry in action, it gives the Holy Spirit an opportunity to work on their hearts and minds.

One word of caution: do not be overly reliant on the bulletin because not all parishioners read it. To achieve good attendance at an event, for example, it needs to be promoted by other means in addition to the bulletin.

Overview

Goal: To establish regular communication about the Vocation Ministry and its activities through the parish bulletin

Target Audience: Parishioners
Lead Time: 2 weeks
Implementation: Easy

People

External Leaders: None
VM Leaders: Priest, director, communications coordinator
Additional Volunteers: None

Resources

Materials Needed: None
Funds Needed: None
Number Expected: N/A
Promotion: Coordinate with person in the parish who is in charge of bulletin, for timing and process
Resources Available: Pre-written blurbs in English and Spanish relevant to each Sunday's scripture readings are available at www.vocationministry.com

Instructions

1. Consult the priest/pastor for input on implementation and for his blessing.
2. Determine who will coordinate the activity.
3. Contact the parish bulletin coordinator for details on process and timing.
4. Submit information on each vocation activity to be placed in the bulletin.
5. Following each event, submit a recap, with a picture if possible, and thank all involved in making it a success.
6. In between activities, include pre-written blurbs that provoke thought about vocations.

Notes:

—Many parishes pay companies to create their bulletins. These companies offer a variety of bulletin covers for a given weekend. For example, for Priesthood Sunday, they might have several covers to choose from that artfully bring attention to this event. Contact the parish bulletin coordinator for information.

—Consider having the blurbs submitted in other languages frequently spoken in the parish.

—Sample blurbs to begin publicizing an upcoming event:

Pre-Event Blurb: Pope Francis is coming! Look for Pope Francis' cutout at the Ministry Fair next weekend. Stop by the ministry booth and take a picture with our pope. We would love to share information about activities of the Vocation Ministry with you.

Happy Birthday to priest: The Vocation Ministry wishes Father John a very Happy Birthday! You are such a gift to our parish, and we are truly blessed to have your guidance and wisdom! Thank you for your "Yes" to the priesthood!

Sunday, February 2: Today we rejoice and celebrate World Day for Consecrated Life. Over the years, many men and women have chosen to live out their baptismal vocation by professing the evangelical counsels of poverty, chastity, and obedience. They do this by joining a religious congregation, a secular institute, or through private vows. Please sign a card at the back of the church to pray for the consecrated from our parish. Please continue to pray for the consecrated in our world and ask God to bless our Church with others who will dedicate their lives to God's service.

Marriage Event: The Vocation Ministry is presenting an event on the vocation of MARRIAGE on October 2nd at 6:30 p.m., in the auditorium. Refreshments will be provided. John and Patty Smith will give an inspiring talk on discerning and living marriage as a vocation, a call to holiness, and life-giving fruitfulness. This event is free of charge.

—Sample blurbs to include in lieu of events:

The Epiphany: God chose us before the world began to be holy. God has chosen each person in Christ for a particular vocation. If he may be calling you to be holy through a vocation to the priesthood or consecrated life, contact your Office of Vocations by phone (xxx-xxx-xxxx) or email (xxxxx@xxx.xxx).

Sixth Sunday of Easter: Those who love me will keep my word. Is your love for the Lord leading you to grow in holiness as a priest or in the consecrated life? Contact your Office of Vocations by phone (xxx-xxx-xxxx) or email (xxxxx@xxx.xxx).

ACTIVITY 17

Discerner's Packet

We know there are youth at every parish discerning their vocation, but most do not have the information needed to make informed choices. A Vocation Ministry can easily help by placing this information at their fingertips in the church book rack, website, or youth room.

Overview

Goal: To increase awareness of vocation resources for a discerning parishioner

Time of Year: Year-round

Target Audience: Discerning parishioners

Lead Time: 2 months

Implementation: Easy-moderate

People

External Leaders: None

VM Leaders: Priest, director, communications coordinator

Additional Volunteers: None

Resources

Materials Needed: None

Funds Needed: $30 for copies

Number Expected: Up to all discerning parishioners

Promotion: Include blurb in bulletin and newsletter that materials are available, and place packet on church website

Resources Available: See an example at www.vocationministry.com

Instructions

1. Consult the priest/pastor for input on implementation and for his blessing.

2. Determine who will coordinate the activity.
3. Determine which resources should be included in the packet. Suggestions are:

    a. Letter of encouragement

    b. Recommended books, such as *To Save a Thousand Souls*

    c. Recommended websites

    d. Links to videos about the priesthood and religious life

    e. Bible verses about vocations

    f. Priestly and religious contacts at various parishes

    g. Recommendations for parents about activities that foster vocations

    h. Recommendations for discerner about activities in the parish that can help foster a possible vocation

4. Do the proper research to attain pertinent information.
5. Make copies for the church book rack.
6. Publicize in the bulletin and newsletter that the resource is available and post on the church website.
7. Ask the youth ministry if copies can be left in the youth room wherever they may be easily seen.

Notes:

—Take note to receive permission before giving out email addresses or phone number of anyone in the packet, especially priests and religious.

ACTIVITY 18

Promotional Materials

A ministry should use every opportunity to educate parishioners about vocations. Promotional materials such as a priest cut out or button that says, "We Love Our Priests!" can bring joy and inspiration to young and old alike. These materials make great conversation starters, too. For example, one day a priest was driving behind a car with a "We Love Our Priests!" bumper sticker on it. When he stopped at the next light, he ran up to the driver's window and said, "I love your bumper sticker! Thank you!"

You never know who may see a button or bumper sticker while discerning a vocation! Buttons, pamphlets, posters, and banners are all visible ways to encourage parishioners to think about vocations beyond the bulletin each Sunday.

Overview

Goal: To bring awareness to vocations and to affirm priests and religious with giveaways, posters, and banners
Time of Year: Any
Target Audience: All members of parish
Lead Time: 1 month
Implementation: Easy

People

External Leaders: None
VM Leaders: Priest, director, communications coordinator
Additional Volunteers: None

Resources

Materials Needed: Basket for presentation (optional)
Funds Needed: Varies; bumper stickers and buttons can run $2-5 each, posters $40+ each, and banners $100.
Number Needed: Varies
Promotion: N/A
Resources Available: Links to vendors and downloadable banners at www.vocationministry.com

Instructions

1. Consult the priest/pastor for input on materials and quantities, and for his blessing.
2. Determine which promotional materials make the most sense for the parish, and how many are needed. Consider price breaks for certain quantities.
3. Create or order promotional materials.
4. Give one of each to each member of ministry to display or wear, especially when working for vocations in any capacity.

5.   Hand out materials at special events.

6.   Display posters and/or banners the week of each event in a prominent location.

Notes:

—Because of the cost, consider first asking parishioners if they will wear a button and/or display a bumper sticker the materials when offering them one. This cuts down on the number that end up in the trash.

—Stock up for special events such as parish festival, Priesthood Sunday, National Vocation Awareness Week, and receptions.

PHASE II

ACTIVITY 19

Festival Table

Many Catholic parishes have an annual festival to raise funds and build fellowship. This is the perfect opportunity to introduce parishioners to the Vocation Ministry and explain its mission of promoting and affirming vocations within the parish.

At the festival, a ministry can focus on the interaction between priests, religious, seminarians, and the parishioners through games of tug-of-war, arm wrestling, hula-hoop contests, and vocation jeopardy. These activities show that priests and religious can be playful and joyful.

Overview

Goal: To increase awareness of and interest in vocations and the Vocation Ministry with a presence at the parish festival
Time of Year: During parish festival
Target Audience: Every parishioner in attendance
Lead Time: 3 months
Implementation: Moderate to complex

People

External Leaders: Parish festival coordinator
VM Leaders: Priest, director, parish festival coordinator, communications coordinator
Additional Volunteers: 2-6 adults who enjoy working with children to staff booth; adults and/or youth ministry for booth set-up and cleanup

Resources

Materials Needed: Promotional materials; candy and/or prizes; booth table, chairs, and decorations
Funds Needed: $150-500 depending on promotional materials, candy, and prizes
Number Expected: Up to the entire parish

Promotion: Begin publicizing booth through bulletin, newsletter, and website at least one month prior to event.

Resources Available: Links to vendors of cardboard cutouts of a priest, sister, or religious brother, buttons, banner, and bumper stickers at www.vocationministry.com

Instructions

1. Consult the priest/pastor for input on implementation and for his blessing.
2. Determine who will coordinate the activity.
3. Determine the scope and theme of booth (activities, prizes, candy, etc.).
4. Obtain all materials for booth.
5. Publicize the booth through bulletin, newsletter, website, and Mass announcements at least two months prior to the event. Set up, staff, and clean up booth.
6. Thank all those who stopped by the booth in the bulletin, adding a picture or two to share this special event with the parish at large.
7. Send a thank you note to each external leader, expressing the ministry's gratitude for their help in the success of the activity.

Notes:

—Having free candy and handouts available will attract much attention from the children and their parents, especially if booths at the festival require money to participate. With an interested audience, the ministry can start to introduce vocations to all in the parish.

—Youth who need service hours are a great resource for a ministry.

—Sample booth hand-outs:

> Miraculous Medals
> Vocation pamphlets and brochures
> "We Love Our Priest" buttons
> "Priests Rock!" buttons
> "We Love Our Priests!" bumper stickers

—Sample booth activities:

> Priest and nun cutouts for parishioners to place their heads through (purchase at www.vianneyvocations.com)
> Tug-of-war

Arm-wrestling

Hula-hoop contest

Pin-the-Miter-on-the-Bishop

Vocation Jeopardy (see activity on page 150)

—Consider using this opportunity to have parishioners sign a card or gift for a priest for Priesthood Sunday, an upcoming birthday, or ordination anniversary.

ACTIVITY 20

Ministry Fair Table

The Ministry Fair, sometimes known as a Stewardship Fair, is a perfect opportunity to spread the word about the Vocation Ministry and recruit new members.

You can draw volunteers to the cause by having a well-decorated table and asking outgoing members to speak enthusiastically about the work of the ministry.

So many parishioners, especially if the ministry is new, know so little about vocations; thus, simply being present at the fair increases awareness of vocations.

Overview

Goal: To gain new Vocation Ministry members and evangelize about ministry programs with a presence at the parish ministry fair

Time of Year: During parish ministry or stewardship fair

Target Audience: Parishioners

Lead Time: 4-6 weeks

Implementation: Moderate

People

External Leaders: None

VM Leaders: Director, activity coordinator or special events coordinator

Additional Volunteers: Ministry members to staff the booth

Resources

Materials Needed: Ministry promotional flier, tablecloth, religious items to beautify the table, sign-in sheet for prospective members to fill in contact information, vocations banner (optional), cut-out of Pope or other eye-catching items

Funds Needed: $20 to make copies of promotional flier

Number Expected: Varies, depending on size of parish

Promotion: parish normally publicizes the ministry fair; Vocation Ministry members should personally invite people to visit the booth

Resources Available: Flier and sign-up sheet at www.vocationministry.com

Instructions

1. Determine who will coordinate the activity.
2. Make sure all ministry members know the date of the fair, with as many committing to attend as possible.
3. Download or create a ministry fair flier and sign-up sheet.
4. Schedule two ministry members to staff the table before and after each Mass.
5. Gather vocational materials, such as general literature from the book rack, information for a discerner, or prayer cards, to distribute at the fair.
6. Decorate the table before the first Mass of the weekend.
7. Download or create a sign-in sheet.
8. Greet parishioners enthusiastically, and let them know about the Vocation Ministry's work and how they can help.
9. In the bulletin, thank all those who stopped by the booth, adding a picture or two to share this special event with the parish at large.

Notes:

—Be prepared to offer possible volunteers options for helping the ministry. Some people may want to commit to attending all the meetings and activities, but others may only be able to help when an extra set of hands is needed. Having two sign-up sheets may aid in keeping track of the two types of volunteers better than placing them all on the same sheet.

World Day for Consecrated Life

Consecrated life is a blessed gift given when Jesus Christ chooses a person to answer his great call of love in a distinct and special way. He requests that person leave behind features of the world such as marriage and wealth to serve their brothers and sisters. Consecrated life is a vocation, like marriage and priesthood, where men and women seek an intimate relationship with Christ.

These men and women are witnesses to the world that we are all ultimately called to unite with Christ, choosing to live out their baptismal vocation by professing the evangelical counsels of poverty, chastity, and obedience. They do this by joining a religious congregation, a secular institute, or through private vows.

The U.S. Conference of Catholic Bishops states that World Day for Consecrated Life "is attached to the Feast of the Presentation of the Lord in February... This Feast is also known as Candlemas Day, the day on which candles are blessed symbolizing Christ who is the light of the world. So too, those in consecrated life are called to reflect the light of Jesus Christ to all peoples. The celebration of World Day for Consecrated Life is transferred to the following Sunday in order to highlight the gift of consecrated persons for the whole Church."[13]

Overview

Goal: To bringing awareness to and prayers for those consecrated to Christ
Time of Year: World Day for Consecrated Life (early February)
Target Audience: Parishioners, especially the youth
Lead Time: 2 months
Implementation: Easy/moderate

People

External Leaders: None
VM Leaders: Priest, director, activity coordinator, youth minister, special events coordinator, communications coordinator

---

13 "World Day for Consecrated Life." www.usccb.org. N.p., n.d. Web. 27 June 2014.

Additional Volunteers: 2-12 adults and/or youth ministry for reception set-up and cleanup

Resources

Materials Needed: Posters of consecrated, banner, and informational materials and/or prayer cards to be placed near parish entrances; see Reception on page 189

Funds Needed: Varies, depending on reception, materials offered, and $30-50 stipend for each consecrated man or woman who attends

Number Expected: Up to entire parish

Promotion: Begin publicizing through bulletin, newsletter, website, and Mass announcements at least a month prior to event

Resources Available: Posters of consecrated may be available from Diocesan Office of Vocations; banner can be downloaded at www.vocationministry.com

Instructions

1. Consult the priest/pastor for input on implementation and for his blessing.
2. Determine who will coordinate the activity.
3. Discuss ideas for this event, determining the scope of the event (promoting through bulletin, banners, and such and/or asking consecrated men or women, which includes religious sisters and brothers, to speak after Mass, at reception, at a school assembly, and/or at youth ministry event)
4. If the speakers will address only the youth at an event planned by the youth minister, consult with them to see how the Vocation Ministry can help.
5. Ask the parish liturgy coordinator to place a prayer petition for consecrated men and women in the Prayers of the Faithful in the liturgy on the weekend of World Day for Consecrated Life.
6. Publicize through the bulletin, newsletter, website, and Mass announcements at least one month prior to event.
7. If available, obtain posters of the consecrated from the Office of Vocations to place at each parish entrance.
8. Glue posters to a sturdy board or put them in frames and place them on easels in an area of high visibility.

9. Ask parishioners to pray for each of the consecrated men and women.
10. If desired, plan reception (see activity on page 189).
11. Make the consecrated men and women feel at home in your parish, no matter what their role is that day.
12. Give the speakers a card of appreciation and a stipend after the reception, Masses, or youth ministry function.
13. Set up for, enjoy, and clean up after the reception.
14. In the bulletin, thank all those who attended, adding a picture or two to share this special event with the parish at large.

PHASE III

ACTIVITY 22

Called By Name

The words of the prophet Isaiah are still powerful today: "I have called you by name; you are mine" (Isaiah 43:1). We know God is calling thousands of men and women to serve him as priests and sisters. It is the privilege and responsibility as adult Catholics to help identify, encourage, and support those who are being called to serve the Lord.

Called By Name, developed and promoted by Serra, is recommended by the U.S. Bishops' Committee on Vocations. This successful program invites men and women, 18 years of age or older, to consider a vocation as a priest, sister, or brother.

Many seminarians say that the final nudge to contact the vocation director was simply being asked, by their pastor, parent, grandparent, or any Catholic adult, if they had considered the priesthood. It is crucial that parishes actively support and promote future generation of priests and religious sisters and brothers to serve a growing Church, hungering for Christ in the Eucharist.

Overview

Goal: To solicit from parishioners names of those considered good candidates for the priesthood or religious life, and to hold information and discernment event(s) for those nominated

Time of Year: Any two consecutive weekends of Mass

Target Audience: Men and women ages 18+

Lead Time: 4 months

Implementation: Complex

People

External Leaders: None

VM Leaders: Priest, director, youth minister, activity coordinator, communications coordinator

Additional Volunteers: None

Resources

Materials Needed: Nomination cards

Funds Needed: $20 for copies of nomination card

Number Needed: One for each adult in parish

Promotion: Begin preparing parishioners through bulletin, newsletter, website, and Mass announcements at least one month prior to event

Resources Available: Link to timeline, posters, scripts, and meeting plans, and extremely detailed outline at www.vocationministry.com

Instructions

1. Consult the priest/pastor for input on implementation and for his blessing. His involvement will be necessary.
2. Determine who will coordinate the activity.
3. Determine the scope of the program—whether to hold discernment events at the parish or lead the candidates to the diocese; whether to plan Mass around vocations both weekends or only the first; whether to include vocations in the religious education programs leading up to and/or on the weekend of the event; and who will speak at the Masses (parish clergy, religious, seminarians, or other religious in formation).
4. If using outside speakers to introduce the program at Mass (seminarians or religious), either ask the pastor or contact the Office of Vocations to recommend speakers.
5. If leading the candidates to diocesan discernment events, schedule the date at least three months prior to diocesan discernment programs.
6. Create or order nomination cards, seminarian and vocation posters, and any other planned vocation literature.
7. For the weekend Masses introducing the program, ask the priest to address vocations in the Homily, Prayers of the Faithful, and music.
8. For the weekend Masses introducing the program, ask the Religious Education Director to include vocation awareness in the lesson plan.
9. Inform parishioners about the event through the bulletin, newsletter, website, and Mass announcements for at least one month prior to the event.

10. Place vocation materials such as literature and posters of seminarians and consecrated at the main entrance and exits of the church before the first weekend Mass.

11. During Mass the first week, inform parishioners of the characteristics of an ideal candidate for the priesthood and religious life. Also include the information and nomination cards in bulletin, newsletter, and website updates for those unable to attend.

12. Ask parishioners to take a nomination card home, pray the vocation prayer on the card throughout the week, prayerfully consider names of good, potential candidates, write the name(s) on the nomination card, and turn them in the following Sunday or mail them to the parish office.

13. Choose one of the two following options for Mass the next weekend.

    a. Collect nomination cards only.

    b. Provide another opportunity for another to speak about vocations and to invite others to consider the call. If priests or seminarians spoke the previous weekend, perhaps ask a religious to speak. Coordinate the Homily, Prayers of the Faithful, and music to address vocations. Collect nomination cards.

14. Sort the nomination cards for the priests.

15. Invite all persons nominated to attend an informational program either at the parish or through the diocese Office of Vocations, where participants learn about the call and life of ministry as a priest or religious, have an opportunity to seek answers to their questions, and are invited to explore discernment processes further.

Follow-up:

1. Parish priests and any designated staff members examine the names of individuals submitted by parishioners.

2. The pastor sends a letter to each individual considered to have qualities needed as a future religious or priest, with the good news that his/her name has surfaced as a result of the Called By Name program.

3. The Called By Name coordinator follows up the pastor's letter with a phone call encouraging that person to either attend a parish or diocesan discernment event, asking permission for the Diocesan Vocation Office to contact them, assuring them that you will pray for them to discern their vocation, no matter which vocation he/she may choose.
4. Provide the Office of Vocations with the names and contact information of those parishioners who gave permission to share that data.
5. Publish a thank-you blurb from the parish priests and staff in the bulletin for everyone's participation. Consider providing the number of names that surfaced, but do not publish the names that surfaced. It is still early in the process for the potential discerners.

Notes:

—This is an advanced program. Don't implement it until the parish has developed a strong sense of vocations and the ministry is full of volunteers.

—Consider conducting a parish discernment program like the Melchizedek Project for those identified during Called by Name.

—A more personable approach could be accomplished, depending on the pastor's wishes, by reaching out to all those in the parish who work with the youth to identify those who seem to be called or open to that call. Then discernment groups for male and female of all ages could be formed and overseen by the Vocation Ministry and the pastor.

ACTIVITY 23

Fish Fry for Vocations

Numerous councils of the Knights of Columbus sponsor a Fish Fry each Friday of Lent at their parishes. Using one of those Fish Fry Fridays to promote vocations is a great opportunity. Priests, religious men and women, professed and in formation, and seminarians can enjoy food and drink while they mingle with parishioners.

Moreover, these guests can share their short vocation testimony with those in attendance. This activity inspires the parishioners—young, old, married, or single—by allowing them to see the joy exuded from those already following God's call.

Overview

Goal: To increase awareness about living out a vocation to parishioners and to give the priestly and religious guests an opportunity to interact with parishioners, share their vocation testimony, and receive a free meal and encouragement

Time of Year: Lent

Target Audience: Priests, religious men and women, professed and in formation, seminarians and parishioners

Lead Time: 2 months

Implementation: Moderate

People

External Leaders: Knights of Columbus leader

VM Leaders: Priest, director, Knights of Columbus liaison, seminarian liaison, communications coordinator

Additional Volunteers: Ministry members to greet seminarians

Resources

Materials Needed: Gift card to movies, coffee shop, or restaurant

Funds Needed: Varies, depending on how many seminarians attend

Number Expected: Varies, depending on number of guests invited to share testimony; up to as many as all parishioners

Promotion: Begin publicizing through bulletin, newsletter, website, and Mass announcements at least one month prior to event

Resources Available: Invitation and thank-you note to seminarians at www.vocationministry.com

Instructions

1. Consult the priest/pastor for input on implementation and for his blessing.
2. Determine who will coordinate the activity.
3. Ask the Knights of Columbus in your parish to consider dedicating one Lenten Fish Fry to vocations.

4. Download or create an invitation to the event and send to various priests, religious men and women professed and in formation, and seminarians, asking them to prepare their short vocation testimony and to RSVP a week before the event.

5. Inform parishioners about the event through the bulletin, newsletter, website, and Mass announcements at least one months prior to the event.

6. Buy the appropriate number of gift cards to give each speaker who attends. These could be a $10 gift card to a local restaurant, movie theater, or book store.

7. Coordinate with Knights of Columbus about the order of events.

8. Arrange for a microphone to be available for the speakers to use.

9. Greet each speaker who attends and introduce them to the Knights of Columbus.

10. Walk the speakers through the food line, making sure they are not charged for food.

11. Introduce speakers to parishioners throughout the night.

12. Introduce the speakers using the microphone. As an alternative, a parish priest, deacon, or Knight of Columbus can introduce the guests.

13. Ask each speaker to share his/her vocation testimony. The length of each testimony should be determined by the number of seminarians present.

14. Thank the priests, religious men and women, and seminarians for coming and give them their gift cards.

15. Send a formal thank-you note to all speakers and the Knights of Columbus and thank all those who attended and the Knights of Columbus council again in the bulletin, adding a picture or two to share this special event with the parish at large.

Notes:

—This venue can also be used to bring awareness to the parishioners about the discernment process, number of seminarians/religious in formation from the diocese, and upcoming ordination dates.

—Consider providing an opportunity for married couples to give their testimony as well.

ACTIVITY 24

To Save a Thousand Souls

Father Brett Brannen's book *To Save a Thousand Souls* is the definitive guide for men discerning the priesthood. It explains the priesthood, the discernment process, and what seminary is like. It is now the standard "catechism for discernment" throughout the country, with more than 100 U.S. dioceses ordering books. Young men attest that this easy-to-read book answers most of their questions about discerning their vocation, and many seminarians cite its important role in their decision-making process.

Every Vocation Ministry should have copies of this book on hand to present to a young man who is seriously discerning the priesthood. Furthermore, every ministry member should read the book to gain knowledge of the discernment process for these young men.

Overview

Goal: To provide each discerner a copy of the book *To Save a Thousand Souls: A Guide to Discerning a Vocation to Diocesan Priesthood*
Time of Year: Any
Target Audience: Young men seriously discerning a vocation to the priesthood
Lead Time: 1 month
Implementation: Easy

People

External Leaders: None
VM Leaders: Priests, director, activity coordinator
Additional Volunteers: None

Resources

Materials Needed: *To Save a Thousand Souls,* by Father Brett Brannen
Funds Needed: $17 per book
Number Needed: One for each discerner
Promotion: N/A
Resources Available: Purchase books at www.vianneyvocations.com

Instructions

1. Consult the priest/pastor for input on implementation and for his blessing. Ask if he and any other priests would be willing to distribute books to discerners, either one-on-one or at a discernment event.
2. Determine who will coordinate the activity.
3. Purchase books.
4. Give 2-3 books to each priest in your parish for distribution.
5. Contact www.melchizedekproject.com to ask about obtaining free copies if the books will be used for discernment groups.
6. Check with each priest every six months to restock if necessary.

Notes:

—Distributing and using this book in a discernment group is a good follow-up to Called by Name (see page 107).

───────────── **ACTIVITY 25** ─────────────

Melchizedek Project

The Melchizedek Project is a small discernment group for teenagers and young adults. Materials for the group are provided for free via www.melchizedekproject.com. To guide discussion, members use *To Save a Thousand Souls*, the definitive guide to discerning priesthood, by Father Brett Brannen.

The groups meet for 90 minutes seven times per semester to discuss key aspects of discernment, such as prayer, celibacy, seminary, and more. This can be a standalone activity or a great follow-up for individuals whose names emerged from the Called By Name program (see activity on page 107).

Overview

Goal: To encourage serious discernment through an extended program
Time of Year: Any, preferably at the beginning of the semester
Target Audience: Young men discerning a vocation to the priesthood
Lead Time: 3 months

Implementation: Complex

People

External Leaders: Possibly the Diocesan Vocation Director or local chaplains from high schools or colleges

VM Leaders: Priest, director, activity organizer, special events coordinator, communications coordinator

Additional Volunteers: None

Resources

Materials Needed: Leader guide, *To Save a Thousand Souls*, posters and postcards (optional);

Funds Needed: Materials are free. Cost of refreshments varies.

Number Needed: One book for each discerner, one leader guide for each leader

Promotion: Invite known discerners; post free posters around parish (optional); begin publicizing through bulletin, newsletter, website, and Mass announcements at least one month prior, send bulletin blurb and announcement to surrounding parishes, advertise on local Catholic radio for free, place blurb in the diocesan newspaper.

Resources Available: Visit www.melchizedekproject.com

Instructions

1. Consult the priest/pastor for input on implementation and for his blessing.
2. Determine who will coordinate the activity.
3. Request a free startup packet at www.melchizedekproject.com.
4. Determine the dates of the 14 sessions, seven per semester.
5. Determine who should lead each session. Possibilities include the vocation director, priest, chaplain, pastor, parochial vicar, youth minister, lay campus minister, or student leader. In some situations, a hybrid may be best. For example, the vocation director could lead the first meeting, then the students could carry the discussion forward.
6. Plan reception (see activity on page 189).

7. Decide how to promote this activity. If the activity is conducted after Called by Name, contact the young men who were nominated to personally invite them to participate.

8. Once the number of attendees is known, coordinate with the parish facilities director to reserve a place for the meetings and reception, if needed.

9. At least two weeks before the first meeting, order the appropriate number of needed books from www.melchizedekproject.com.

10. Provide all meeting leaders a copy of the book and a leader guide to read before the first meeting.

11. Set up for, enjoy, and clean up after the reception.

12. Consider calling or emailing reminders to each attendee before every session.

Notes:

—Note that the discussion questions for the group are included as an appendix in *To Save a Thousand Souls*.

—The more points of communication, the better. To increase the likelihood of attendance, personally invite the young men face-to-face and follow-up with an email, Facebook messages, a phone call reminder, and a text message the day of the meeting.

ACTIVITY 26

Invite Seminarians to Special Events

Seminarians work diligently, attending classes, studying, praying, and attending official functions. An active Vocation Ministry can give these young men an opportunity to unwind and enjoy fellowship with one another and parishioners. Many seminarians attend seminary far away from their home dioceses, so this event could provide much-needed support.

Invite the seminarians, from either the parish or diocese, to join in the entertaining events of parish life which gives them a glimpse into the positive facets of being a diocesan priest. Furthermore, the parishioners can get to know these young men and encourage them while studying for the priesthood. These events lift up the seminarians while promoting vocations at the same time.

Overview

Goal: To get to know, support, and increase awareness about seminarians to parishioners by inviting them to a parish event

Time of Year: Any special event, such as fundraisers or celebrations

Target Audience: Seminarians, parishioners

Lead Time: 2 months

Implementation: Moderate

People

External Leaders: None

VM Leaders: Priest, director, seminarian liaison, communications coordinator

Additional Volunteers: Ministry members to greet seminarians

Resources

Materials Needed: Invitation and thank-you note

Funds Needed: Amount to cover the cost of seminarians attending

Number Expected: 2-6 seminarians, up to all parishioners

Promotion: Inclusion in the bulletin at least two weeks in advance and an announcement to parish weekend before; send invitation and thank-you note via email or mail

Resources Available: None

Instructions

1. Consult the priest/pastor for input on implementation and for his blessing.
2. Determine who will coordinate the activity.
3. Decide as a ministry to which event seminarians will be invited to attend.
4. Invite the seminarians four weeks before event via email or mail, asking them to RSVP a week before the event.
5. Purchase the appropriate number of tickets for the attending seminarians, if needed. This money can be donated by ministry

members or others in the parish or can come out of the ministry/ parish budget.

6. Greet every seminarian who attends and introduce them to parishioners throughout the evening.

7. Give the seminarians space to enjoy their evening.

8. In the bulletin, thank the seminarians for coming and all those who attended, adding a picture or two to share this special event with the parish at large.

Notes:

—This can easily be adapted to include those in religious formation to become brothers and sisters. They all need to feel parishioners' appreciation and to enjoy a night out every once in a while.

PHASE IV

ACTIVITY 27

Inspirational Exhibit

Most Catholics are in need of inspiration from time to time when striving for holiness, the first vocation. A ministry can provide an exhibit that encourages parishioners to live as Christ calls each of us to live. The subject can be about miracles, angels, saints, or anything that will promote the faith in some way to parishioners. Sometimes a "traveling exhibit" will make its way around the country. While these types of traveling exhibits don't always feature a direct message about vocations, it can be inspiring to see great figures throughout Church history living out God's plan.

Overview

Goal: To bring awareness to some facet of vocations by bringing a traveling exhibit to the parish or area

Time of Year: Any, especially in conjunction with another vocation event

Target Audience: Parishioners

Lead Time: 4-6 months

Implementation: Complex

People

External Leaders: Exhibit contact

VM Leaders: Priest, director, activity coordinator, communications coordinator

Additional Volunteers: 6-8 adults to decorate and set up, staff, and cleanup exhibit

Resources

Materials Needed: Exhibit, decorations for tables, tables (if the exhibit does not include easels), fliers that explain exhibit flow, 8 1/2 x 11 plastic tray; for reception, see activity on page 189

Funds Needed: Varies, depending on amount and type of publicity, decorations, and reception

Number Expected: 50-300, depending upon publicity and size of parish

Promotion: Inclusion in bulletin and weekend Mass announcements at least one month in advance, place fliers around campus, send bulletin blurb and announcement to surrounding parishes, advertise on local Catholic radio for free, place blurb in the diocesan newspaper

Resources Available: Link to possible exhibits at www.vocationministry.com

Instructions

1. Consult the priest/pastor for input on implementation and for his blessing. He may know of exhibit possibilities.
2. Determine who will coordinate the activity.
3. Cover the event in prayer from beginning to end.
4. Search for a traveling exhibit by contacting the diocese, The Real Presence, or researching Catholic exhibits on the internet.
5. Find out what kind of space is needed for the exhibit and coordinate with the parish facilities coordinator on a location at the parish. Often, not all displays in the exhibit have to be utilized, so space should not be an issue. Plan for enough space for attendees to walk through the exhibit comfortably.
6. Determine scope of the event, including reception (finger foods or even cookies and coffee could add a sense of reception and lend itself to more community building), decorations (such as a standing crucifix and some flowers at the start of the exhibit), and music (classical music or Gregorian chants can add to the ambiance).
7. Begin promoting the event at least a month in advance through the local Catholic radio station and newspaper (contacting each two months prior to event), surrounding parishes, and in the bulletin, newsletter, website, and Mass announcements.
8. Schedule ministry members or other volunteers to pick up, deliver, unpack, and set up the exhibit (the night before the opening, if possible); to staff the exhibit, with two volunteers present at all

times to answer questions and guide attendees to the restrooms and food, if available; and to clean up and return exhibit.

9. Set up for, enjoy, and clean up after the exhibit.
10. Send a thank you note to each external leader, expressing the ministry's gratitude for their help in the success of the activity.
11. In the bulletin, thank all those who attended, adding a picture or two to share this special event with the parish at large.

Notes:

—The exhibit can stand alone or be added to an event like National Vocation Awareness Week.

—This activity may be accomplished in conjunction with other nearby parishes.

—A relic of a saint could also be displayed for veneration.

—Consider inviting children from the parish school and religious education classes to tour the exhibit.

Personal Ministry Highlight

How the exhibit came about

God was in the midst of all the work we did when coordinating the efforts with many groups of the archdiocese for World Day of Prayer for Vocations. One day I called Elsie, who I thought was the leader of the Lay Missionaries of Charity, only to find out that new leadership had taken over the previous month.

What happened next was astounding. Elsie said she knew why I had contacted her instead of the current leader, which intrigued me thoroughly. She revealed that an exhibit of Blessed Mother Teresa that was touring the United States would be in Houston that week, and that we were meant to have it at Saint Mary's Seminary for World Day of Prayer for Vocations. This was more than coincidence.

The exhibit, in English and Spanish, included 78 different panels of pictures and words on the life of Mother Teresa. This beautiful display is a wonderful reflection of her works and the continual fruits of her labors and prayers. All those in attendance had the opportunity to write their petitions to ask for her intercession, which were then taken to Calcutta and placed on Mother Teresa's Tomb. Most importantly, a first-class relic of Mother Teresa accompanied the exhibit for veneration and blessings.

I heard countless stories of praise and inspiration from those who walked through the Blessed Mother Teresa Exhibit. What a great gift that was to all of us. Priests, sisters, seminarians, and children young and old were touched by her story and by being in the presence of her relic. God was intimately involved in this addition to the World Day of Prayer for Vocations, letting us all see in those panels Blessed Mother Teresa living out her vocation.

The following year, we still did not have an exhibit two months from the date of the event, so we prayed that the Holy Spirit would inspire us and that we would be receptive to his will for this event. That week, I called Father Dat Hoang, vocations director for the archdiocese at the time, to discuss the invitations. He said he had met a woman who told him of a Vatican exhibit of the Miracles of the Eucharist, which they house and host. Not only did we have our exhibit, we had it in time to promote it in the invitation. God has great timing!

ACTIVITY 28

Speaking Events on Marriage

One of the functions of the Vocation Ministry that is often forgotten is to encourage strong marriages—as a call to holiness for the two joined as one and as an encouragement to married couples to become open to their children considering a priestly or religious vocation. Remembering to reinforce marriage as a vocation will strengthen the family unit, the parish, and the Church, and bring about more vocations.

A ministry should take every opportunity to emphasize that marriage, although witnessed to young people every day by their parents, is a sacrament conveying the bond of love between Christ and his people and should be discerned as strongly as the other vocations of the Church.

For example, young men and women considering marriage should seek God's will regarding the matrimonial life well before the wedding day. A large percentage of high school girls already have their wedding day planned out, not taking into account God's plan for their lives. If each Vocation Ministry educates the youth with regards to discerning marriage, imagine how much lower the divorce rate could be in the Catholic Church and society at large.

When answering the question, "What is marriage?" Pope Francis said, "It is a true and authentic vocation, as are the priesthood and the religious life. Two Christians who marry have recognized the call of the Lord in their own love story: the vocation to form one flesh and one life from two, male and female."[14]

Overview

Goal: To share information about the vocation of marriage and to support marriage with a special event

Time of Year: Any

Target Audience: Singles; dating, engaged, and married couples

Lead Time: 4-6 months

Implementation: Complex

People

External Leaders: Event speakers

VM Leaders: Priest, director, activity coordinator, special events coordinator, communications coordinator

Additional Volunteers: 8-10 ministry members and other adults to help organize and staff event

Resources

Materials Needed: Promotional fliers, donation baskets, see Reception on page 189

Funds Needed: $500-1,000, depending on advertising, food, and speaker stipend

Number Expected: 50-300 parishioners, depending on parish size

---

14 http://www.usccb.org/issues-and-action/marriage-and-family/marriage/promotion-and-defense-of-marriage/upload/Pope-Francis-1st-anniversary-Marriage-bulletin.pdf

Promotion: At least one month prior to event, begin publicizing in
 bulletin, newsletter, website, and Mass announcements; place fliers
 around campus; send bulletin blurb and announcement to surrounding parishes; advertise for free on local Catholic radio; place blurb in
 diocesan newspaper
Resources Available: See sample flier at www.vocationministry.com

Instructions

1. Consult the priest/pastor for input on implementation and for his blessing.
2. Determine who will coordinate the activity.
3. Determine which couple(s) to invite to speak at event.
4. Invite the couple(s) to speak, making sure they will focus on living their vocation in holy matrimony, and coordinate possible dates and time for the event.
5. Reserve an auditorium or community center area large enough to hold the expected crowd.
6. Plan the reception (see activity on page 189).
7. Begin promoting the event at least a month in advance through the local Catholic radio station and newspaper (contacting each two months prior to event), surrounding parishes, and in the bulletin, newsletter, website, and Mass announcements.
8. Request a check to pay the speaking couple from the budget if they are not donating their time.
9. Schedule ministry members or other volunteers to staff the event, including set-up, greeting attendees, food service, taking video and/or photos the event, and cleanup.
10. Set up for, enjoy, and clean up after the event.
11. Send a thank you note to each couple, expressing the ministry's gratitude for their help in the success of the activity.
12. In the bulletin, thank the speakers and all those who attended, adding a picture or two to share this special event with the parish at large.

Notes:

—While a reception with food requires money, time and effort, it also
 draws a crowd, especially if the reception is around dinnertime. One

way to offset costs is to provide a way for attendees to make a donation, either at the entrances or tables.

Personal Ministry Highlight

About a year into our ministry work, we hosted an event to promote marriage as a vocation. Parishes around Saint Cecilia Catholic Church, along with our own parishioners, were invited to learn how to have a holy courtship and marriage.

Matt Regitz, long-time youth minister at Prince of Peace Catholic Community in Houston, and his wife Stephanie, shared "Marriage on Purpose: Put a Ring on It!" In their presentation, they revealed that their courtship was rooted in Christ, and that with their strong faith, they have weathered many storms in their marriage. Stephanie and Matt shared their about the tragedy of losing their first-born daughter, Mary Clare. Their trust in God's will in their lives, during tragedy and fortune, inspired all in the audience to cling to Christ in their own marriage.

We were amazed by the turnout. Several hundred people attended, including engaged and married couples as well as singles. Matt and Stephanie even changed a last-minute activity they had planned because of the number of people present. It was a great problem to have.

We gave an honorarium to Matt and Stephanie to share their story, but you may have one or more couples in your own parish who can share their testimony without much cost. It is important to highlight these virtuous examples of sacramental marriages at every parish.

CHAPTER 6

YOUTH ACTIVITIES

Pope Saint John Paul II said to the youth at World Youth Day in 2002: "The future is in your hearts and in your hands. God is entrusting to you the task, at once difficult and uplifting, of working with him in the building of the civilization of love."[15]

The Vocation Ministry's role in forming youth to rise to the challenges of building that civilization is to continually propose the possibility of priesthood and religious life. Providing opportunities for youth to interact with those who are already living out their vocation shows them real-life men and women who are happy as a priest or religious. For example, playing vocation-themed games with the younger children helps them think about vocations in a fun way.

The youth-related activities listed here should inspire each ministry to embrace any activity that will help open the hearts of the children and teens in the parish to hear God's call in their lives.

---

15 http://www.vatican.va/holy_father/john_paul_ii/speeches/2002/july/documents/hf_jp-ii_spe_20020727_wyd-vigil-address_en.html

PHASE I

The Newman Connection

Almost 80% of college students stop practicing their faith at some point during college, with only 15% actually seeking a college campus ministry on their own. In an effort to help more students become involved in campus ministry, the Newman Connection offers a simple solution.

First, this program gathers the names of graduating seniors, the college of choice, and where it is located. Then, the Newman Connection passes along these names to the campus ministers at the respective universities. Finally, they provide individual students with the contact information of the campus minister, along with other details to help them get involved once they arrive on campus.

In this way, the student and campus minister have a good opportunity to connect.

Vocation Ministries in every parish have a clear and simple motivation for helping keep older teens and young adults practicing their faith. The more they are going to church and participating in college campus ministry, the more they are open to hearing God's call. According to a recent survey, almost 20% of respondents said they first considered a vocation to the religious life between ages 19-24. Each ministry should reach out to their youth ministers to do their part to keep our young adults practicing their Catholic faith.

Overview

Goal: To connect the teens and young adult college students with campus ministers

Time of Year: In April or May before a high school senior leaves for college

Target Audience: Graduating high school seniors in the parish

Lead Time: 1 month

Implementation: Easy

People

External Leaders: N/A
Ministry Members Needed: Priest, director, youth minister
Additional Volunteers: N/A

Resources

Materials Needed: Computer and contact information for graduating high school seniors
Funds Needed: None
Number Expected: Varies
Promotion: N/A
Resources Available: Connect at www.newmanconnection.com

Instructions

1. Consult the priest/pastor for input on implementation and for his blessing.
2. If the priest approves of this activity, ask if he would like to ask the youth minister, a paid staff member, to implement this program or have the director or another member of the ministry do so.
3. If the priest wants a ministry member to contact the youth minister, decide who will approach him/her.
4. Introduce Newman Connections to the youth minister. All that is needed is the name of the college, its location, and student information to make this program a success.
5. When you have the youth minister's approval, ask if he needs help inputting the data into the Newman Connection website.
6. Send a thank you note to the youth minister, expressing the ministry's gratitude for his help in the success of the activity.

Notes:

—Consider hosting a meal for all high school seniors, where the ministry can celebrate the seniors and acquire their college choices.

PHASE II

ACTIVITY 30

Altar Server Recognition at Mass

Most priests' first memories of serving the Lord are as altar servers. A national survey of men being ordained priests found that three-quarters of new priests were at one time altar servers.[16] A Vocation Ministry can organize altar server recognition at Mass that reinforces in young people the joy of serving the Lord.

Overview

Goal: To recognize and show appreciation for the work of altar servers during Mass
Time of Year: Any
Target Audience: Altar servers, parishioners
Lead Time: 6 weeks
Implementation: Easy

People

External Leaders: None
VM Leaders: Priest, director, activity coordinator, communications coordinator
Additional Volunteers: Ministry members to greet altar servers

Resources

Materials Needed: Certificates for altar servers (optional)
Funds Needed: $30-50 for printing certificates
Number Expected: Up to number of altar servers in parish
Promotion: Publicize through bulletin, newsletter, website, and Mass announcements at least one month prior to event
Resources Available: Find a downloadable template by visiting www.vocationministry.com

---

16 "New priests Younger, Were Altar Servers, Lectors, Carry Debt." www.USCCB.org. n.p., 17 May 2012. Web. 10 July 2014.

Instructions

1. Consult the priest/pastor for input on implementation and for his blessing.
2. Determine who will coordinate the activity.
3. Determine, with priest's input, at which Mass altar servers will be recognized—either the servers in attendance at every mass or during a specific Mass, such as the anniversary of the altar server's service or a designated day.
4. Include in the bulletin the altar servers designated for each Mass and each altar server's anniversary of service (optional).
5. Create a certificate for each altar server.
6. After receiving a blessing from the priest, present a certificate to each altar server, either on the designated day or on the anniversary of service.
7. In the bulletin, thank all those who volunteer as altar servers, adding a picture or two to share this special event with the parish at large.

Notes:

—Consider requesting that at each Mass all altar servers stand to be recognized and receive a blessing, as well.

—Instead of, or in conjunction with the certificate, an altar server medal or trading card can be given to the servers.

ACTIVITY 31

Art Contest

Promoting vocations can and should be fun! Using a variety of ways to bring awareness to vocations, especially to the youth, will keep all parishioners eager to learn more from the Vocation Ministry.

An art contest allows children of all ages to focus on some aspect of vocations using any medium they like. The idea is to encourage the youth to think about vocations in a new way. These art projects may cover any number of topics including "Saying Yes to God!", "Let Us Remember We

Are in the Holy Presence of God," "Jesus Came to Serve," or another creative theme.

Overview

Goal: To raise awareness of and educate about vocations through art
Time of Year: Any, especially during National Vocation Awareness
Week
Target Audience: Students in parish school and/or religious education
classes, youth in confirmation preparation classes, parish families
Lead Time: 2 months
Implementation: Moderate

People

External Leaders: Principal and/or religious education director
VM Leaders: Priest, director, communications coordinator, school liaison, activity coordinator, youth minister, faith formation liaison
Additional Volunteers: None

Resources

Materials Needed: Place ribbons (optional), program (optional)
Funds Needed: Varies depending on scope of event
Number Expected: Varies, depending on the number of children in the
parish school, youth ministry, and parish at large.
Promotion: Publicize student art show through bulletin, newsletter,
website, and Mass announcements at 2 weeks prior to event
Resources Available: Download advertisement for art contest, "Saying
Yes to God" at www.vocationministry.com

Instructions

1. Consult the priest/pastor for input on implementation and for
    his blessing.
2. Determine who will coordinate the activity.
3. Consult with the appropriate leader (principal, religious education director, or youth minister). Ask for permission, the most

appropriate age group, the best time for the activity, and who should be involved in the planning.

4. Provide a time for art to be created. If promoted by the parish school and/or religious education classes, supplies may be provided by the school/church.

5. Depending on age of participants and availability of judges, consider whether art is judged—based on categories or alignment with themes—or only displayed. If judged, be sure all winning artwork is marked with an indicator of place (ribbon, stars marked with places, etc.), notify winners and, if possible, gather winners near their artwork and take their pictures, which can be used for promotion in a bulletin or newsletter.

6. Display the art at the school or parish. If other activities are already planned for National Vocation Awareness Week, the display of art by parish children or teens is an effective, supplemental way to increase parish engagement and vocation visibility.

7. If a separate event is desired, plan a special time to allow families and other parishioners to enjoy the art. If resources allow, include a simple reception (see page 189).

8. If planning a separate event, begin publicizing the event through the bulletin, newsletter, website, and Mass announcements at least two weeks in advance.

9. Create a simple program for the event that lists participants and winners.

10. Set up for, enjoy, and clean up after the event.

11. After the event send a note of appreciation to the youth minister, principal, or religious education director for their help and cooperation.

12. In the bulletin, thank all those who participated, adding pictures of the winners with their artwork to share this special event with the parish at large.

ACTIVITY 32

Children's Mass Kit

M any priests fondly remember "playing" Mass when they were growing up. They possibly used sheets as vestments and Vanilla Wafers as hosts.

Some large families have enough siblings to provide altar servers, lectors, and a few parishioners in the pews to play along. This valuable activity is easy to put into place and will create a perfect opportunity for the Holy Spirit to plant more seeds of holiness.

Overview

Goal: To raise awareness of the priesthood as a vocation by providing a
   Mass kit for children to play with at home
Time of Year: Any, could be launched during National Vocation Awareness Week or Priesthood Sunday
Target Audience: Parish children
Lead Time: 1 month
Implementation: Easy

People

External Leaders: None
VM Leaders: Priest, director, activity coordinator, communications
   coordinator
Additional Volunteers: None

Resources

Materials Needed: Mass kit
Funds Needed: $60-150 per kit commercially
Number Expected: Varies, depending on the number of children in the
   parish
Promotion: Publicize through bulletin, newsletter, website, and Mass
   announcements two weeks prior to kit availability
Resources Available: Links to ordering kit at
   www.vocationministry.com

Instructions

1. Consult the priest/pastor for input on implementation and for his blessing.
2. Determine who will coordinate the activity.
3. Discuss details of the activity, such as whether to buy a Mass kit or have one made, how to conduct sign-ups (call a point person or conduct a specific sign-up weekend), how long kit can be used by one family, and how to coordinate the transfer of the kit.
4. Obtain the kit.
5. Create publicity flier of children "playing" Mass.
6. Begin publicizing through bulletin, newsletter, website, and Mass announcements two weeks prior to kit availability.
7. Conduct sign-up for kit.
8. Communicate with families by email or phone to remind the family to pick up and return the kit at an appointed time and place.

Notes:

—Consider including a costume habit of a nun with the Mass kit to promote religious life and plastic rosaries to promote holiness.

ACTIVITY 33

Christmas Carols

Christmastime is filled with wonder and joy, especially for children. Having a priest or religious sister or brother visit classrooms of the parish school or religious education classes to sing Christmas carols shares the happiness that those living out their vocation have with the children. When a child can see that Christmas brings out such marvel in those serving Christ, they too can ponder the possibility of a religious vocation.

Overview

Goal: To bring joy to the children and provide an opportunity for them to interact with a pastor or priest

Time of Year: Advent season

Target Audience: Students in parish school and/or religious education classes

Lead Time: 1 month

Implementation: Easy

People

External Leaders: School principal and/or religious education director

Ministry Members Needed: Priest, director, school liaison, and activity coordinator

Additional Volunteers: None

Resources

Materials Needed: Christmas carols

Funds Needed: $10-15 to make copies of music

Number Expected: Varies, depending upon the size of the classes

Promotion: None

Resources Available: Link to Christmas carol lyrics can be found at www.vocationministry.com

Instructions

1. Consult the priest/pastor for input on implementation and for his blessing. If he is not available, ask him or for suggestions of who could lead the students in Christmas carols.
2. Determine who will coordinate the activity.
3. Consult with the appropriate leader (principal or religious education director), before moving forward, for permission and to determine the best day/time for the activity.
4. Invite a priest or religious to lead the carols.
5. Send a thank you note to each external leader, expressing the ministry's gratitude for their help in the success of the activity.

Notes:

—This activity may be led by a deacon, too.

—If the priest is not open to the idea at that time, you have at least planted a seed that may bring results later.

—Consider asking the youth minister if this can be done at a parish youth ministry event with either the middle or high school students during confirmation preparation.

ACTIVITY 34

Classroom Visits

All Catholic schools employ lay teachers now, so having priests, seminarians, and religious men and women visit the school and religious education classes is incredibly important. Exposure to those living a radical life for Christ allows the children to see their joy and interact with them, hear their vocation testimony, and ask them questions about their vocation call. From personal experience, this activity has led many young people to discern their vocations in a more profound way. Many children are enthralled with meeting sisters, especially those in habits, and this often leads to a high-energy Q&A session.

Overview

Goal: To raise awareness of and educate children about vocations by having priests, religious, and/or seminarians visit classrooms

Time of Year: Any (and often!), especially during National Vocation Awareness Week and World Day for Consecrated Life

Target Audience: Students in parish school and/or religious education classes

Lead Time: 4-6 weeks

Implementation: Moderate

People

External Leaders: School principal and/or religious education director

Ministry Members Needed: Priest, director, school liaison, youth minister, activity coordinator

Additional Volunteers: Priests, religious brothers and sisters, seminarians, religious men and women in formation, married couples to visit classrooms

Resources

Materials Needed: None

Funds Needed: Possible stipends for any religious or priest attending, gift cards can be purchased for those in formation or married couples who attend

Number Expected: Up to entire parish school, and religious education classes

Promotion: N/A

Resources Available: N/A

Instructions

1. Consult the priest/pastor for input and for his blessing.
2. Determine who will coordinate the activity.
3. Determine the scope of the visits (all classrooms—religion classes at parish school and/or religious education classes).
4. Receive permission from appropriate leaders and discuss how many guests can visit and the timing of the visits in the school year.
5. Invite the appropriate number of guests to visit classrooms (priests, seminarians, men and women in religious formation, sisters, and married couples).
6. Greet the guests and introduce them to the person in charge, whether that is the principal or religious education director.
7. After the event, give each guest his or her stipend check or gift card, along with a note of appreciation for attending.
8. Thank all those who attended in the bulletin and parish school newsletter, adding a picture or two to share this special event with the parish at large.

Notes:

—Ideally, no more than 2-3 persons would go into each classroom at one time so that all have an opportunity to speak.

—Consider having a conference room as a reception area with small finger foods and drinks during breaks.

—Keeping the different vocations separate while visiting each classroom will allow for less confusion among the students. For example, the sisters should tour separately from the priests.

—Furthermore, a nice gesture after the event is to have the youth in attendance to draw cards or write notes of thanks to each guest at the assembly.

ACTIVITY 35

Panel Discussion

One way to showcase all types of vocations to the youth in the parish is by holding a vocations panel discussion. The main idea is to show the children examples of men who love the priesthood, joyful religious men and women, and married couples who strive to keep Christ at the center of their marriage. As often as possible, the children need be in contact with models of holiness to gain inspiration.

Overview

Goal: To raise awareness of and educate about vocations by hosting a panel discussion

Time of Year: Any, especially during National Vocation Awareness Week and World Day for Consecrated Life

Target Audience: Students in parish school and/or religious education classes, youth in confirmation preparation classes

Lead Time: 3-4 months

Implementation: Moderate

People

External Leaders: School principal and/or religious education director

Ministry Members Needed: Priest, director, school liaison, activity coordinator, seminarian liaison, youth minister, youth representative, and affirmation coordinator

Additional Volunteers: Priests, sisters, deacons, religious brothers and sisters, seminarians, religious men and women in formation, and married couples to participate in panel

Resources

Materials Needed: Stipend checks from parish and/or gift cards, microphone(s), and chairs

Funds Needed: Varies, depending on number of participants. $30-50 stipend/gift card to each participant, especially religious or clergy; $15-20 gift cards for those men and women in religious formation or for a married couple

Number Expected: Varies, depending on the size of assembly

Promotion: N/A

Resources Available: Questions for panel discussion at www.vocationministry.com

Instructions

1. Consult the priest/pastor for input on implementation and for his blessing.
2. Determine who will coordinate the activity.
3. Consult with the appropriate leader (principal, religious education director, or youth minister) about the idea, asking the best time for the activity (after weekly school Mass, during an assembly with certain classes present, or for certain grades in a youth ministry) and who should be involved.
4. Contact guests (priests, religious, seminarians, married couples) to sit on the panel.
5. Determine which questions to ask the panel, keeping in mind the target audience ages. Ask the youth representative to provide perspective on which topics would be well received. Share the questions with the guests ahead of time to hear more thoughtful answers.
6. As a standard practice, request $30-50 stipend checks for the clergy and religious sisters or brothers to offset the cost of time and travel. Purchase $15-20 gift cards to a coffee house, restaurant, or movie theater for seminarians or married couples.
7. Have a chair for each guest and at least one microphone available.
8. Ask at least two ministry members to attend the event to greet the guests and introduce them to the person in charge, who will introduce them to the assembly.

9. After the event, give each guest his or her check or gift card, along with a note of appreciation.

10. Send a thank you note to each external leader, expressing the ministry's gratitude for their help in the success of the activity.

11. In the bulletin, thank all those who attended, adding a picture or two to share this special event with the parish at large.

Notes:

—Ideally, no more than 4-5 persons would be on the panel so that all have an opportunity to speak.

—If the parish has a seminarian studying in a different city, or even Rome, consider using technology such as Skype to bring him into the discussion.

—A nice gesture after the event is to have the youth in attendance draw cards or write notes of thanks to each guest at the assembly.

──────────────── ACTIVITY 36 ────────────────

Reunion Mass and Reception

Children's eyes light up when they meet a priest or religious who attended their parish school and/or parish. These real-life vocation stories of calling and transformation provide unique perspective to the children of the parish community.

The Vocation Ministry can introduce those men and women who have become priests and religious to those children at a school Mass or to all families at Sunday Masses.

For instance, at the first attempt our ministry made at a reunion Mass, we were able to find two priests, one sister, and a transitional deacon to speak to the students at a school Mass. The transitional deacon revealed that he was the least-likely student to become a priest.

His shyness led to great anxiety about speaking in front of others. His honesty resonated with the students. He said, "It is amazing what God can do when we open our hearts to him!"

The next year a bishop who graduated from the school gave the homily, and when he shared his feelings of being in the first graduating class of the school in 1959, the children were amazed.

Furthermore, the adults of the parish see and hear these holy men and women and may open their hearts further to the possibility of one of their own children becoming a priest or religious. After the Mass, consider allowing the guests to reconnect at a small reception, which is a meaningful way to lift them up and say, "Thank you!"

Overview

Goal: Honor clergy, religious sisters and brothers, and those in formation for the priesthood or religious life who graduated from the parish school or were a member of the parish growing up

Time of Year: Any, especially during Priesthood Sunday, World Day for Consecrated Life, and National Vocation Awareness Week

Target Audience: Students in parish school, families in the parish

Lead Time: 4-6 months

Implementation: Complex

People

External Leaders: School principal

VM Leaders: Priest, director, school liaison, seminarian liaison, affirmation coordinator, special events coordinator

Additional Volunteers: Priests, sisters, deacons, religious brothers and sisters, seminarians, or religious men and women in formation who either graduated from the parish school or who were once parishioners of the parish

Resources

Materials Needed: Stipend checks from parish, gift cards; for Reception (see activity on page 189)

Funds Needed: Varies, depending on reception and number of guests. $30-50 stipend/gift card to each religious or clergy; $15-20 gift cards for those men and women in religious formation or for a married couple; $100-200 for food and drink at the reception.

Number Expected: Varies, depending on the size of school and
reception

Promotion: Publicize in bulletin, newsletter, website, school newsletter,
and Mass announcements at least one month prior to event

Resources Available: See pictures of like activities at
www.vocationministry.com

Instructions

1. Consult the priest/pastor for input on implementation and for
    his blessing.
2. Determine who will coordinate the activity.
3. Consult with the principal, asking for his/her permission, the
    best date and time for the activity, who should be involved in the
    planning, and where the event will take place.
4. Gather the names of bishops, priests, sisters, religious brothers
    and sisters, seminarians, and religious men and women in forma-
    tion who either graduated from the parish school or who were
    once parishioners of the parish.
5. Good sources of information on possible guests are the Office of
    Vocations, a local seminary, school board members, parishioners,
    and the Internet (search for "alumni" and the school name).
6. Contact all alumni and any other guests (principal, assistant prin-
    cipal, teachers of the alumni, and other staff) at least two months
    in advance, asking for an RSVP two weeks prior to the event.
7. Ask the pastor which guests should speak at Mass, either during
    the homily or at the end of Mass.
8. Plan the reception (see activity on page 189). Take into account
    the time of day of the Mass to determine the type of appropriate
    food to serve.
9. As a standard practice, request $30-50 stipend checks for the cler-
    gy and religious sisters or brothers to offset the cost of time and
    travel. Purchase $15-20 gift cards to a coffee house, restaurant, or
    movie theater for seminarians and those in religious formation.
10. Ask at least two ministry members to attend the event to greet
    the guests and introduce them to the person in charge, who will
    introduce them to the assembly.
11. Set up for, enjoy, and clean up after the reception.

12. Give each guest his or her check or gift card, along with a note of appreciation.
13. Send a thank-you note to each external leader, expressing the ministry's gratitude for their help in the success of the activity.
14. In the bulletin, thank all those who attended, adding a picture or two to share this special event with the parish at large.

Notes:

—If guests are traveling from far away, increasing their stipend may be appropriate.

ACTIVITY 37

National Vocation Awareness Week

National Vocation Awareness Week was instituted in 1976 by the United States bishops. It is a time set aside for parishes to foster a culture of vocations to the priesthood and religious life. Since 2014, it has been held during the first full week of November.

Pope Francis, in his November 2013 apostolic exhortation, *Evangelii Gaudium*, underlined the continued need to build a culture of vocations: "The fraternal life and fervor of the community can awaken in the young a desire to consecrate themselves completely to God and to preaching of the Gospel. This is particularly true if such a living community prays insistently for vocations and courageously proposes to its young people the path of special consecration." [17]

National Vocation Awareness Week provides a numerous opportunities for an active Vocation Ministry to have a parish-wide impact each year.

Personal Ministry Highlight

A pastor, parochial vicar, or deacon who is loved by the children is the number one advocate for the Vocation Ministry.

---

17 http://www.vatican.va/evangelii-gaudium/en/index.html

Encourage him to visit classrooms on a regular basis and reach out to him for help when implementing other activities at the school.

Our parochial vicar Father Victor Perez was treated as a rock star when he walked the school's halls. He visited various classrooms regularly so that students could get to know him. He played soccer with the elementary students at recess once a week. He also led a walking Rosary once a week for the middle-school students. During Christmastime, he brought his guitar and sang Christmas carols with every class. The children loved him and responded to his kindness. You can bet the children listened when Father Victor gave his vocation testimony or spoke to them about praying to know their own calling.

Father John Cahoon, our pastor of 12 years, also communicated easily with the students at school Masses. I love watching him pass the microphone around, asking the children questions during his homilies. This was such a great opportunity for him to interact with them in a public way. He gave his vocation testimony at Mass, inspiring them to seek God's will in their own lives.

If you do not have a priest who feels comfortable around children, arrange a meeting with the school liaison and the school principal several months in advance to coordinate activities that would educate the children about vocations and inspire them to explore their own vocation.

We are fortunate at Saint Cecilia to have a parish school that educates over 600 students, from pre-kindergarten through eighth grade. With that blessing, we feel a great responsibility to create an environment where each child can think and pray about what his or her vocation might be.

After three months of ministry work, we undertook a week of vocation activities at the school. Father Victor asked for a whole week of activities and the principal agreed. The sky was the limit!

The possibilities for National Vocation Awareness Week are endless. Here are a few ideas that have been particularly fruitful for our school children:

Year One

Preparation

A few weeks in advance, Father Victor and I met with the religion teachers. The week before, we sent the teachers lesson plans and activities. Some resources can be found at serraus.org. A high-quality curriculum supplement for grades K-12 is available at www.vocationlessons.com.

Monday

- Religion teachers introduced vocations to the students.
- To promote the idea of vocations, we handed out 600 trading cards featuring local seminarians, each with a name and photo on one side and a prayer on the other (see activity on page 158). All year long we heard stories of classes that had students trading the cards!
- We gave out another 1,000 seminarian trading cards to children in religious education class, youth ministry, and those at Sunday Masses.

Tuesday

- Sisters from different orders held a panel discussion (see activity on page 139) for the 4th-8th graders and visited all classrooms. One sang before sharing her vocation testimony. Another shared an amazing talk about her challenging childhood in Vietnam.

Wednesday

- We held a special reunion Mass and reception (see activity on page 172) for priests and religious alumni from Saint Cecilia Catholic School. Two priests, one sister, and a transitional deacon eagerly shared testimony of when they walked those same halls, proving that God calls all types of people to work in his vineyard.
- Six seminarians served at Mass and visited all 40 classrooms afterwards. They played games with children at re-

cess and ate in the cafeteria. The students were enamored with all of them.

Friday

- The vocation director from the Archdiocese of Galveston Houston shared his moving vocation testimony with the 4th-8th graders (see activity on page 137).
- He also showed the 18-minute vocation DVD, Fishers of Men (see activity on page 152), a major resource in a vocational recruitment project launched by the U.S. Conference of Catholic Bishops (USCCB).
- A class set of Vision Magazine (www.vocationnetwork.org) was given to each middle school religion teacher to use for various assignments.

The week lit a fire for vocations in our school. After having such success the previous year, we were given permission to return the following year.

Year Two

Monday

- Three ordination classmates spoke to the 5th-8th graders about the priesthood, showing a video of their ordinations and taking questions.

Tuesday

- A class set of Vision magazines was given to each middle school religion teacher.
- A religious brother, deacon and three sisters visited classrooms throughout the day, inspiring the children wherever they went.
- Table Tents (see activity on page 148), which contained conversation starters about vocations for families to use when at the dinner table, were given to students and families throughout the parish and school.

Wednesday

- At a second reunion Mass, an alumnus who became a bishop provided a homily about being in the first graduating class of the school. A retired auxiliary bishop and two other alumni priests concelebrated at the school Mass.

Thursday

- We held the first parish-wide art contest, "Saying Yes to God!" (See activity on page 131).

Friday

- Two consecrated women spoke to the 4th-8th graders about living life for Christ. They received thought-provoking questions about the difference between a consecrated woman and a nun. Everyone at the assembly, adults and children alike, learned a great deal.

These activities can take place at any time during the school year, but it works well to hold them in conjunction with National Vocation Awareness Week or another widely-recognized time to promote vocations.

ACTIVITY 38

Table Tents

Promoting vocations should not occur only on parish grounds. Education and conversation about vocations between parents and children at home is crucial to keep everyone thinking about God's will.

Take-home table tents can include an explanation about vocations from the catechism and a question for each day of the week that families can discuss, and allow all members of the family time to reflect on their present or future vocation.

Overview

Goal: To raise awareness of and educate about vocations by providing families with table topics on vocations

Time of Year: Any, especially during National Vocation Awareness Week

Target Audience: Students in parish school and/or religious education classes, youth in confirmation preparation classes, parish families

Lead Time: 2 months

Implementation: Moderate

People

Leaders: Principal and/or religious education director

VM Leaders: Priest, director, school liaison, activity coordinator, youth minister, faith formation liaison

Additional Volunteers: None

Resources

Materials Needed: Table tents

Funds Needed: $100 to make copies of the table tents and cover letters.

Number Expected: Varies, depending on the number of children in the parish school, youth ministry, and parish at large.

Promotion: N/A

Resources Available: Table tent and cover letter in both English and Spanish for parents at www.vocationministry.com

Instructions

1. Consult the priest/pastor for input on implementation and for his blessing.
2. Determine who will coordinate the activity.
3. Consult with the appropriate leader (principal, religious education director, or youth minister) about the idea, asking for permission that they be sent home to parents, the most appropriate age group, the best time for the activity (after weekly school Mass, during an assembly with certain classes present, or for certain grades in a youth ministry) and who should be involved in the planning.
4. Download and print the table tents and cover letters and deliver to the appropriate person for distribution.
5. After the event send a note of appreciation to the youth minister, principal, or religious education director for his or her help and cooperation.

6. Communicate in the bulletin and the school newsletter about the initiative, explaining the benefits to all.

Notes:

—This activity could be executed on its own or in conjunction with a speaker on vocations.

ACTIVITY 39

Vocations Jeopardy

Whether at a parish festival or panel discussion, whenever the Vocation Ministry needs to have a fun way introduce vocations, play a game of Vocations Jeopardy! The object of this game is not only to have fun, but also to challenge the youth to think more openly about various vocations. It is a quiz game played just like the television show Jeopardy!

Overview

Goal: To raise awareness and educate about vocations through a fun game

Time of Year: Any, especially in conjunction with activities at vocations booth at parish festival

Target Audience: Children in parish school, religious education classes or youth in confirmation preparation classes, children in parish at large

Lead Time: 1 month

Implementation: Easy to moderate

People

External Leaders: Principal, religious education director, or parish festival coordinator, depending on where activity takes place

VM Leaders: Priest, director, activity coordinator, school liaison, youth minister, faith formation liaison

Additional Volunteers: 2-3 adults with organizational and interpersonal skills who enjoy children

Resources

Materials Needed: Copy of the game, 2 or 3 classic service bells, candy
   for prizes
Funds Needed: $30 for candy prizes, $10 for classic service bells
Number Expected: Varies depending on attendance
Promotion: As needed with primary event
Resources Available: Visit www.vocationministry.com to find Voca-
   tion Jeopardy

Instructions

1. Consult the priest/pastor for input on implementation and for
    his blessing.
2. Determine who will coordinate the activity.
3. Decide on the target audience. This could be played at a parish
    festival or given to teachers at parish school or parish religious
    education classes and/or youth minister.
4. If the game is only to be played at the parish festival, follow these
    steps:
    a. Download one copy of the game that can be played by
    children of any age. Highlight the questions to signify which
    are easy, moderate, and difficult for easy adaptation to the
    audience.
    b. Purchase candy and bells (optional).
    c. Set up the table and ask children if they want to play.
    d. Allow children to play against each other, either ringing
    a bell or hitting the table when they want to answer the
    question.
    e. Consider giving one piece of candy for one correct answer
    and a small bag of candy for three correct answers.
5. If game is to be played within an educational setting, follow these
    steps:
    a. Consult with the appropriate leader (principal, religious
    education director, or youth minister) about the idea, asking
    for permission, the best time for the activity, what grade(s)
    will participate, and who should be involved in the planning
    of the activity.

b. Download and print the appropriate number of copies.

c. Decide if candy will be provided as prizes. If so, purchase the candy.

d. Distribute the game, bells (optional), and candy, if applicable, to the appropriate person.

e. Send a note of appreciation to the principal, religious education director, or youth minister for his or her help and cooperation.

Notes:

—Including a tidbit of information about the parish priests and/or deacons in each bag of candy is a great way to add more depth to this fun activity.

—Adults can participate in this activity, too. Of course, ask the harder questions! Have fun!

ACTIVITY 40

Vocation Video

Some youth will be inspired by a talk or by praying a rosary with a priest, and others will feel moved by seeing a well-made video highlighting a vocation, or even one aspect of a vocation. The potent visuals and musical scores of some of the more dramatic videos can imprint strong feelings about a vocation.

Overview

Goal: To raise awareness of and educate about vocations by showing a video

Time of Year Any, especially during one of the yearly major vocation events

Target Audience: Students in parish school and/or religious education classes, youth in confirmation preparation classes

Lead Time: 2 months

Implementation: Moderate

People

External Leaders: School principal and/or religious education director

VM Leaders: Director, activity coordinator, school liaison, youth minister, faith formation liaison, youth representative

Additional Volunteers: None

Resources

Materials Needed: Vocation video

Funds Needed: Varies, depending on the purchase of a DVD

Number Expected: Varies, depending on the size of assembly

Promotion: N/A

Resources Available: Inspirational and educational videos about the priesthood and religious life are at www.vocationministry.com

Instructions

1. Consult the priest/pastor for input on implementation and for his blessing.
2. Determine who will coordinate the activity.
3. Consult with the appropriate leader (principal, religious education director, or youth minister) about the idea, asking the best time for the activity (after weekly school Mass, during an assembly with certain classes present, or for certain grades in a youth ministry) and who should be involved in the planning.
4. Discuss with the ministry, school official, and youth representative which video to show. Keep in mind what technology is available. For example, if the Internet is not accessible, a physical copy of a video must be shown, so a TV and player must be available.
5. Keeping in mind the target audience ages and time allowed, select a video. Here is a list of videos, the running time of each video, and the appropriate ages for each, to help you make that decision:

   Priests (Inspirational):

   Fishers of Men: 18:22 (6th & up)

   Heroic Priesthood: 11:45 (6th & up)

   Priests of Steel: 1:33 (all ages)

   The Catholic Priesthood: 2:59 (all ages)

Priests (Instructional):
Why Priesthood? with Fr. John Muir by Life Teen: 5:10 (9th & up)
Follow Me: Journeys to Priesthood: 13:00 (9th & up)
Five Paths to the Priesthood: 29:55 (9th & up)
How Should I Discern the Priesthood with Fr. Robert Barron: 2:12 (9th & up)
Religious Sisters (Inspirational and Instructional):
Beloved: The Dominican Sisters of St. Cecilia: 2:49 (6th & up)
Light of Love: 1:06:16 (9th & up)
Catholic Sisters in Their Own Words by Life Teen: 5:52 (9th & up)
Jesus Calls Women: 28.40 (12th & up)

6. On the morning of the event, the director, school liaison, youth minister, and/or faith formation liaison should be present to make sure that the video is delivered and working ahead of time.
7. After the event, send a note of appreciation to the principal, religious education director, or youth minister.

Notes:

—This activity could be executed on its own or in conjunction with a speaker on vocations.

ACTIVITY 41

Walking Rosary for Vocations

Priests desire the holiness of all parishioners and want us to bring our sorrow and joy to Jesus through our Blessed Mother. She is always pointing us to her Son. Encouraging the children of the parish school to pray the Holy Rosary with the intention of vocations, and with the help of a priest, and/or religious sister or brother, is a perfect way to lead the youth in seeking God's will in their lives.

Overview

Goal: To bring prayer for vocations, especially one's own vocation, through a walking Rosary at the school or parish
Time of Year: Weekly during the school year

Target Audience: Students in parish school
Lead Time: 1 month
Implementation: Easy

People

External Leaders: School principal and/or religious education director
Ministry Members Needed: Priest, director, school liaison, activity coordinator
Additional Volunteers: None

Resources

Materials Needed: Plastic rosaries
Funds Needed: $20 for rosaries
Number Expected: 20-30, depending upon the size of the school
Promotion: N/A
Resources Available: Link to purchase eye-catching pamphlets on how to pray the rosary for kids at www.vocationministry.com

Instructions

1. Consult the priest/pastor for input on implementation and for his blessing. If he cannot lead the children in a rosary each week, ask him or for suggestions of who possibly could do so.
2. Determine who will coordinate the activity.
3. Consult with the appropriate leader (principal or religious education director) before moving forward for permission and to determine the best time for the activity (whether after weekly school Mass, during recess, or at some other time with only middle school students), and who should be involved in the planning. Ideally the activity will be done weekly so the children become accustomed to praying for our Blessed Mother's intercession.
4. Send a thank-you note to each external leader, expressing the ministry's gratitude for their help in the success of the activity.

Notes:

—This activity may be led by the pastor, a priest, a deacon or religious— whomever is on campus regularly.

—If the priest is not open to the idea at that time, you have at least planted a seed that may bring results later.

—If the principal of the school is not open to the idea yet, ask the priest-pastor if this can be done at a parish youth ministry event with either the middle or high school students during confirmation preparation.

PHASE III

ACTIVITY 42

Altar Server Lunch With Priests

A great way to affirm the servers while allowing them time to get to know the priest is to offer them a meal together. Use any opportunity that the youth can interact meaningfully and joyfully with the clergy.

The food can be as simple as hot dogs or a sit-down meal of the clergy's choice, but make sure to ask the clergy to share some aspect of vocation in their talk with the youth.

Overview

Goal: To recognize and show appreciation for altar servers and to encourage them to consider vocations
Time of Year: Any
Target Audience: Altar servers, priests
Lead Time: 2 months
Implementation: Moderate

People

External Leaders: None
VM Leaders: Priest(s), director, activity coordinator, special events coordinator
Additional Volunteers: 2-6 adults to help during the activity and for lunch set-up and cleanup

Resources

Materials Needed: See Receptions on page 189
Funds Needed: Varies, depending on meal and number of guests attending
Number Expected: All altar servers and priests
Promotion: N/A
Resources Available: N/A

Instructions

1. Consult the priest/pastor for input on implementation and for his blessing.
2. Determine who will coordinate the activity.
3. Determine the date of the event, coordinating with priests to ensure attendance.
4. Plan the luncheon.
5. Invite all priests at least three months prior to the event. Send a save-the-date to the servers two months prior and an invitation 4-6 weeks before the event. Request an RSVP at least one week prior to the event.
6. Set up for, enjoy, and clean up after the luncheon.
7. In the bulletin, thank all those who attended, adding a picture or two to share this special event with the parish at large.

Notes:

—Remember to consider school activities and holidays when scheduling this event.
—Consider pairing this activity with Altar Server Recognition.
—Consider inviting other religious to the luncheon.
—Consider inviting all parish children who may be interested in becoming altar servers.

ACTIVITY 43

Seminarian Trading Cards

To introduce the seminarians to the parish and encourage prayer for each of them, simple trading cards can be created and given to parishioners. They can have the name and photo on one side and a prayer on the other, or more information can be included about each seminarian.

No matter how elaborate the card is, promote prayer and show the children that seminarians are young men finding their way, just like the male youth in the school/parish.

Overview

Goal: To pray for, bring awareness to, and educate about seminarians to the youth of the parish by distributing trading cards featuring these individuals

Time of Year: Any, especially during National Vocation Awareness Week

Target Audience: Children in parish school, religious education classes, youth in middle school youth ministry, and/or confirmation preparation classes

Lead Time: 2-3 months

Implementation: Moderate to complex

People

External Leaders: Principal and/or religious education director

VM Leaders: Priest, director, seminarian liaison, school liaison, youth minister, faith formation liaison

Additional Volunteers: Adult with creativity and computer skills

Resources

Materials Needed: Trading cards

Funds Needed: $100-300, depending on number of cards printed

Number Expected: Varies, depending on the number of children in the parish school, youth ministry, and parish at large, and number of seminarians

Promotion: N/A

Resources Available: Trading card template at www.vocationministry.com (Microsoft Publisher is required)

Instructions

1. Consult the priest/pastor for input on implementation and for his blessing.
2. Determine who will coordinate the activity.
3. Decide on the target audience.
4. Consult with the appropriate leader (principal, religious education director, or youth minister) about the idea, asking for

permission, the best time for the activity, what grade(s) will participate, and who should be involved in the planning. They may see the trading cards as more appropriate for students ages 10 and older, or for all ages.

5. Decide how many and which seminarians to include, taking into consideration the cost of printing. Nine cards fit on a page, with front/back printing required. Color is preferable.

6. Decide how much information about each featured individual to include on each card and solicit the information from the seminarians.

7. Ask a ministry member or volunteer with creativity and computer skills to download and customize the template with the information about the seminarians.

8. Print the needed copies of the trading cards and distribute to the appropriate person.

9. If volunteers for handing out cards are only needed after Masses, schedule ministry members. The Knights of Columbus liaison can also ask his organization to help with this effort.

10. Communicate in the bulletin and the school newsletter about the initiative, explaining the benefits.

11. After the event, send a note of appreciation to the principal, religious education director, or youth minister for his or her help and cooperation.

Notes:

—This activity could be executed on its own or in conjunction with a speaker, especially a seminarian, about vocations.

—This project can be adapted to trading cards for parish priests, which can be given out for Priesthood Sunday; for deacons, which can be given out for Deacon Sunday (see page 185); or for religious men and women in formation, religious sisters and brothers, which could be given out on World Day for Consecrated Life.

PHASE IV

Altar Server Celebration

The children who serve at Mass are at a perfect age for considering their vocations, and the community has a vested interest in their service. So, at least once a year, the ministry should affirm these boys and girls. Though this day can take countless forms, the goal of this activity is to provide encouragement and incentive to keep serving the parish and the Lord in this manner. Remember to make it fun!

Overview

Goal: To recognize and show appreciation for altar servers
Time of Year: Any
Target Audience: Altar servers, parishioners
Lead Time: 2 months
Implementation: Moderate

People

External Leaders: None
VM Leaders: Priest(s), director, activity coordinator, special events
coordinator, communications coordinator
Additional Volunteers: 2-8 adults during the activity, depending on
the number attending, and volunteers or youth ministry to help with
food set-up and cleanup

Resources

Materials Needed: Certificates for altar servers (optional); see Receptions on page 189
Funds Needed: Varies, depending on food, entertainment, and prizes
Number Expected: Up to entire parish
Promotion: Publicize through bulletin, newsletter, website, and Mass
announcements at least one month prior to event
Resources Available: View or download a sample certificate at
www.vocationministry.com

Instructions

1. Consult the priest/pastor for input on implementation and for his blessing.
2. Determine who will coordinate the activity.
3. Meet as a ministry to determine the date of the event, coordinating with priest to ensure his attendance.
4. Determine who will coordinate the activity.
5. Determine whether this will be a breakfast, lunch, or dinner and choose an appropriate menu.
6. Plan the celebration. Some ideas are:
   a. One short vocation talk by a priest and/or sister, depending on the number of girls who will be present.
   b. DJ or music playing for part of the time
   c. Karaoke
   d. Play games such as Vocations Jeopardy (see activity on page 150), Scavenger hunt, pin the miter on the bishop, and piñata (with a vocation twist).
   e. Invite a local Catholic sports hero to inspire the kids to do their best for the Lord in everything they do.
7. Begin publicizing through the bulletin, newsletter, website, and Mass announcements at least one months prior to the event.
8. Include in the bulletin all altar servers' names and their years of service.
9. Create a certificate for each altar server.
10. Set up for, enjoy, and clean up after the reception.
11. In the bulletin, thank all those who attended, adding a picture or two to share this special event with the parish at large.

Notes:

—Remember to consider school activities and holidays when scheduling this event.

—If the ministry needs monetary help to cover food costs, consider requesting donated food from the Knights of Columbus, Women's Club, or local Serra Club.

Altar Server Day at Seminary

The ministry should take every opportunity to have children, especially boys, visit the closest seminary.

Walking on the peaceful and beautiful seminary grounds among inspirational statues of saints, and playing and praying with young men discerning God's will for their lives, can stir at least a thought of their future vocation as a seminarian.

This day, which can vary greatly in execution, serves multiple purposes as it affirms the altar server, educates them on vocations, and normally allows time for personal prayer.

Overview

Goal: To encourage altar servers to consider vocations
Time of Year: Any
Target Audience: Altar servers
Lead Time: 3 months
Implementation: Complex

People

External Leaders: Seminary rector or staff
VM Leaders: Priest, director, activity coordinator, seminarian liaison, communications coordinator
Additional Volunteers: 2+ adults to drive altar servers to seminary, 5-8 members to help with activities at seminary, depending on number of altar servers who attend

Resources

Materials Needed: Vehicles to transport altar servers to/from seminary, all materials needed for games and activities not supplied by seminary
Funds Needed: Varies, depending on reception
Number Expected: All altar servers
Promotion: N/A
Resources Available: N/A

Instructions

1. Consult the priest/pastor for input on implementation and for his blessing.
2. Determine who will coordinate the activity.
3. Consult with a seminary rector or designated staff about the activity.
4. Determine the date of the event while considering any seminary requirements.
5. Plan the day's activities, including the food, with the seminary contact. Some ideas are:

   a. One or two short vocation talks by seminarians

   b. Holy Hour with rosary

   c. Play games such as soccer, basketball, dodge ball, volley-ball, or any sport that includes teamwork where the semi-narians and altar servers could work together

   d. Mass

   e. Lunch or dinner with the seminarians

   f. Tour of the seminary

   g. A talk about a day-in-the-life of a seminarian
6. Invite all altar servers at least six weeks prior to event, requesting an RSVP two weeks prior to the event.
7. Communicate details of the schedule and activities with altar servers at least two weeks prior to the event.
8. Transport altar servers to and from the seminary.
9. Send a thank-you note to each external leader, expressing the ministry's gratitude for their help in the success of the activity.
10. In the bulletin, thank all those who attended, adding a picture or two to share this special event with the parish at large.

Notes:

—If the parish has a large number of altar servers, consider asking their parents to drop them off and pick them up from the seminary, or if budget will allow, rent a bus for the event. The number of altar servers could be limited if funding is an issue.

—Remember to consider school activities and holidays when sched-uling this event.

CHAPTER SEVEN

AFFIRMATION ACTIVITIES

Affirming those who have discerned and are following their vocation is a vital part of the mission of a Vocation Ministry. The giving of oneself to God or to another person is difficult, so a Vocation Ministry should help everyone feel valued in their vocation. The ministry can encourage parishioners to remember those priests, religious, and married couples in the parish who have already answered God's call.

A priest shoulders significant responsibilities. He is tasked with the spiritual leadership of the parish as a whole. He lends guidance and spiritual care to each parishioner, hearing their trials, challenges, sins, and concerns. He is part of their most significant moments in life—their marriages, the births of their children, and the loss of loved ones. He leads staff members and welcomes new members, all in addition to the other administrative work that happens behind the scenes.

Religious brothers and sisters also would benefit from encouragement while serving Christ in their apostolic work or in community. Whether living a contemplative or apostolic life, they do this without the immediate family to provide support and comfort.

Married couples, living in sacramental union, can lean on one another during the roller coaster of life. Though they travel through life together, they still need be affirmed during this journey.

The twelve Affirming activities vary from recognizing the parish priest's ordination anniversary with a small gift or card to the more advanced activities like hosting a parish-wide reception for Priesthood Sunday. Any opportunity for parishioners to thank, support, and share their love and gratitude for those living their vocations should be supported.

PHASE I

Cards and Gifts for Priests

One of the goals of a Vocation Ministry is to lift up the parish priests with affirmation in the form of physical cards and/or gifts. Priests are inundated each day with difficult aspects of their ministry. So often they hear from parishioners who have burdens to share. A simple gesture of kindness and gratitude can make a significant impact on the priest, especially one without family nearby. The ministry can also encourage all parishioners to remember their priests as they do a member of their own family, with love, kindness, and generosity.

Overview

Goal: To encourage and show appreciation for priest
Time of Year: Year-round, especially for birthday, anniversary at parish, ordination anniversary, welcome and farewell to priests, Christmas, and Easter
Target Audience: Ministry members and/or all parishioners
Lead Time: 1 month
Implementation: Easy

People

External Leaders: None
VM Leaders: Director or affirmation coordinator
Additional Volunteers: 1-2 adults to staff card-signing table (optional)

Resources

Materials Needed: Greeting card, small treats (optional)
Funds Needed: $10-$50
Number Expected: N/A
Promotion: Publicize through the bulletin, newsletter, website, and Mass announcements at least two weeks prior to special days, such as priest's birthday, ordination anniversary, anniversary at parish, Easter, Thanksgiving, and Christmas

Resources Available: N/A

Instructions

1. Determine who will coordinate the activity.
2. Obtain a greeting card appropriate for the occasion.
3. Obtain treats such as food, candy, or gift cards to place in a box or basket. His favorite candy and gift cards can be found through the next activity Get to Know Your Priest.
4. Have ministry members sign the card.
5. Provide the opportunity for parishioners to sign the card. (Optional)
6. Present the card and any items to the priest on or before the special day.

Notes:

—Consider adding Spiritual Bouquets to the basket.

ACTIVITY 47

Get to Know Your Priest Questionnaire

Whether a priest has been at the parish one, 10, or 20 years, the majority of parishioners will not be able to say they know him well. Asking the priest to answer a questionnaire and sharing the responses with the parishioners will help those he serves to know him better.

Overview

Goal: To help parishioners get to know their priests better
Time of Year: Any, especially the anniversary of the priest at the parish
Target Audience: Priest, parishioners
Lead Time: 1 month
Implementation: Easy

People

External Leaders: None
VM Leaders: Priest, director, affirmation coordinator

Additional Volunteers: None

Resources

Materials Needed: Questionnaire
Funds Needed: None
Number Expected: N/A
Promotion: As needed with primary event
Resources Available: Questionnaire available at
www.vocationministry.com

Instructions

1. Consult the priest/pastor for input on implementation and for his blessing. Ask if he and other priests would be willing to answer "Get to know you" questions that could be shared with all parishioners, either in writing (bulletin, newsletter, and website) or at a reception.
2. Determine who will coordinate the activity.
3. Download or create a questionnaire. Ask the priest(s) to fill it out at least two weeks prior to needing it. Sample questions:
   - When is your birthday?
   - Where did you grow up?
   - What did your parents do?
   - How many siblings do you have?
   - What is your birth order in the family?
   - What was your favorite book as a child?
   - Who taught you your faith?
   - In which church ministries (such as youth ministry, altar serving) were you involved?
   - Who is your favorite saint(s)?
   - At what age did you start discerning the priesthood?
   - What attracted you to the priesthood?
   - When is your ordination anniversary?
   - When is your anniversary with our parish?
   - What is your favorite church hymn?
   - What is your favorite hobby?
   - What is your favorite sport and/or professional sports team?

- What is your favorite candy?
- What three words would you use to describe yourself?
- How tall are you?
- What type of music do you like to listen to?
- What part of the country do you enjoy most when vacationing?
- What is your favorite food?
- What is your favorite movie?
- What are some of your favorite books?
- What is a fun fact that people might not know about you?

4. Share the answers as planned; for reception see activity on page 189.

Notes:

—This questionnaire can be adapted for religious and deacons, as well.

—Consider sharing one question and answer each week in the bulletin or in a special way at his next reception for a birthday, ordination anniversary, or anniversary at the parish.

—Consider having someone interview the priest and type up his responses.

PHASE II

Priesthood Sunday

E ach fall the Vocation Ministry has the perfect opportunity to guide parishioners in showing their priests appreciation and love. This can take a variety of forms, from a note or prayer to a more complicated reception for all parishioners. No matter the form, assuring the priests of the gratitude of the parish will stay with him long after Priesthood Sunday is over.

Overview

Goal: To celebrate and show appreciation for all priests
Time of Year: Priesthood Sunday (usually last Sunday of October)
Target Audience: Priests, parishioners
Lead Time: 3 months
Implementation: Easy to moderate

People

External Leaders: None
VM Leaders: Priest, director, activity coordinator, special events coordinator, communications coordinator
Additional Volunteers: 5-12 adults to oversee the reception, including set-up and cleanup

Resources

Materials Needed: Cards, banner (optional), reception materials (see activity on page 189)
Funds Needed: Varies, depending on if reception is desired
Number Expected: Up to entire parish
Promotion: Publicize through bulletin, newsletter, website, and Mass announcements at least two months prior to event
Resources Available: Download cards and banner at www.vocationministry.com

Instructions

1. Determine who will coordinate the activity.
2. Meet as a ministry to determine how the ministry would like to celebrate Priesthood Sunday, consulting with priest to ensure his attendance.
3. Coordinate a place for the reception, if desired, with the parish facilities coordinator.
4. Plan the activities surrounding the event, including reception (see activity on page 189). Some ideas are:

   a. A banner announcing a special day to honor the parish priests

   b. Book rack materials in the church narthex that explain priesthood to youth

   c. An announcement at Mass acknowledging the celebration of Priesthood Sunday

   d. A bulletin blurb that specifically recognizes the priests, accompanied by a short biography of their life and priestly service

   e. Ushers offering prayer cards to take home and pray for the parish priests or priests in general

   f. A prayer drive activity, where parishioners of all ages can pledge to pray for vocations

   g. The parish school, religious education classes, and those in youth ministry write cards of affirmation to the priests or create a poster that says "Thank You!" for placement at each entrance to the church.
5. Begin Publicizing the event through the bulletin, newsletter, website, and Mass announcements at least one month prior to the event.
6. Set up for the event the day prior, if possible.
7. Request all ministry members to greet guests and make sure everything runs smoothly.
8. Welcome each priest with a "Happy Priesthood Sunday!" greeting.
9. In the bulletin, thank all those who attended, adding a picture or two to share this special event with the parish at large.

Notes:

—Consider including Cards and Gifts for Priest (see activity on page 166) and/or Spiritual Bouquets (see activity on page 65) with this event.

ACTIVITY 49

Reception for Priest on Special Days

A parish-wide reception can be simple or quite complex depending on the budget and desires of the priest and ministry. Either way, creating the opportunity for the priests to receive so much love from family and parishioners alike will make this labor of love worth all the effort. If the Vocation Ministry is in charge of all priestly receptions, including welcome, farewell, ordination anniversary, Priesthood Sunday and the like, the ministry may want to ask for help from other groups. Actually, this is preferred, as it gives many more parishioners the opportunity to take part in the event. These events are as much about fellowship within the community as they are about the actual reason for the celebration, so don't be afraid to reach out for help, and graciously welcome all who wish to participate.

Overview

Goal: To celebrate and show appreciation for priests and religious
Time of Year: Special occasions (birthdays, anniversary at parish, ordination anniversary, Priesthood Sunday, welcome, and farewell to priests)
Target Audience: Priest, parishioners
Lead Time: 3-6 months
Implementation: Moderate to complex

People

External Leaders: None
VM Leaders: Priest, director, affirmation coordinator, special events coordinator, communications coordinator

Additional Volunteers: Ministry members; 2-12 adults from parish groups and organizations and/or youth ministry for reception set-up and cleanup

Resources

Materials Needed: Event program (optional), see Reception on page 189
Funds Needed: $100-2,000+, depending on reception
Number Expected: 50-400, depending on the size of place for reception and parish
Promotion: Begin publicizing through bulletin, newsletter, website, and Mass announcements at least one or two months prior to event
Resources Available: Pictures of reception ideas at www.vocationministry.com

Instructions

1. Consult the priest/pastor for input on implementation and for his blessing. If he is hesitant, explain the philosophy that this reception provides a real opportunity of meaningful contact with parishioners.
2. Determine who will coordinate the activity.
3. Determine the date of the event, consulting with the priest to ensure his attendance.
4. Determine a budget for the event, consulting with the pastor and/or parish administrator.
5. With the parish facilities coordinator, determine a place for the reception that is available both Saturday for set-up and Sunday for the event.
6. Plan the reception (see activity on page 189), consulting with the pastor/priest to ensure his wishes are granted, to the extent possible.
7. Communicate the date with all parish ministries. Mention this will be a community-wide event and will only happen with everyone's support. Note that another email will be forthcoming with options on how to help. These include donating items or money, serving food or drink, or setting up before or cleaning up after the reception.

8. Provide all ministries and groups with suggestions of a gift for the priest for which all ministries may donate. For a 25th ordination, 50th birthday, or farewell to a beloved priest, a vestment or chalice may be appropriate. Smaller gifts are always welcome, such as a gift certificate for a local Catholic bookstore, a gift card to the movies or favorite restaurant, or cash (he may have large expenses or need a new car).

9. Ask the school principal, religious education director, and/or youth minister to have each student create a "Happy Ordination Anniversary" card or letter, or make one that all students sign.

10. Publicize through bulletin, newsletter, website, and Mass announcements at least two months prior to the event.

11. Meet every few weeks or monthly to discuss arrangements.

12. Find out if the priest has family coming to the reception so that seats may be reserved for them. Consider giving his family the flower arrangement or some token of appreciation for their sacrifices as parents of a new priest.

13. Set up for the event the day prior.

14. Ask all ministry members to greet guests and make sure everything runs smoothly.

15. After the event, give the priest his gifts.

16. Clean up afterward.

17. Write each participating parish ministry or organization a note of appreciation for their contribution.

18. In the bulletin, thank all those who attended, adding a picture or two to share this special event with the parish at large.

Notes:

—A Mass could also be planned before the reception.

—Consider including cards and gifts for priests (see activity on page 166) and/or Spiritual Bouquets (see activity on page 65) with this event.

Seminarian Care Packages

Men in the formation process to become a priest, can sometimes feel as if they are in limbo. They have been called to serve God and his people, and they are eager to do so, but they have not been fully formed and trained to do such important work. They first must experience several years of intense study, continued introspection, and, often, sparse living accommodations. Given these circumstances, they should receive encouragement from those in the parish.

Many seminarians cherish the support of parishioners, the Catholics whom they will serve after ordination. This caring connection with nearby people who share in their faith, appreciate their sacrifices, and encourage their efforts, goes a long way toward inspiring them to remain focused on their mission in life.

Seminarians receive little, if any, spending money from their diocese while in formation, so giving them a care package at Christmas time goes a long way to affirm their sacrifices along the discernment journey. The Vocation Ministry can organize this event so that all parishioners can take part, sharing in showing gratitude, generosity, and kindness toward these young men.

Overview

Goal: To encourage seminarians

Time of Year: Any, especially at Christmas, Easter, and the beginning or end of a semester

Target Audience: Local seminarians, parishioners

Lead Time: 2 months

Implementation: Moderate

People

External Leaders: Office of Vocations staff and seminary rector or staff member

VM Leaders: Priest, director, seminarian liaison, communications coordinator

Additional Volunteers: 2-6 adults or youth ministry to assemble packages

Resources

Materials Needed: Items for packages; containers for packages if assembling through parish

Funds Needed: Varies, depending on donations

Number Needed: One for each seminarian

Promotion: Coordinate with Office of Vocations to prevent duplication of effort; publicize opportunity to donate through the bulletin, newsletter, website, and Mass announcements at least one month prior to event

Resources Available: N/A

Instructions

1. Consult the priest/pastor for input on implementation and for his blessing.
2. Determine who will coordinate the activity.
3. Contact the Office of Vocations staff to determine if they provide this service already.
4. Consult with the seminary rector or a staff member for input on implementation and for his blessing.
5. Determine a day to present packages and the number of care packages needed.
6. Ask parishioners to donate items for the care packages.
7. Assemble care packages, either at the Vocation Office, seminary, or parish.
8. Deliver or assist in delivering care packages.
9. Send a thank-you note to each external leader, expressing the ministry's gratitude for their help in the success of the activity.
10. Thank all those who donated in the bulletin, adding a picture or two to share this special event with the parish at large.

Notes:

—Even small gifts can be meaningful, given that many seminarians exist on a small monthly stipend, if any at all.

—International seminarians may especially benefit from encouragement and small gifts.

—Sample items for care packages: gift card to the movies, local coffee shops, restaurants, office supply stores, grocery stores, etc.; thank you cards; stamps; printer paper; facial tissue; highlighters; pens and pencils; post-it notes; index cards; legal pads; dividers; staples; mints; candy.

PHASE III

Seminarian Cards of Affirmation

S eminarians are in formation for years, taking tests, writing essays, and learning the practical sides of being a priest for God's people. Some young men hail from faraway lands such as South America, Africa and Asia. When asked how hard it was for his family that he left them in Guatemala to study at a United States seminary, one seminarian said that, "It is extremely difficult, but when a seminarian leaves his family, God takes his place." Even with this sentiment, each seminarian, no matter where they are from, needs to be encouraged with intangible prayer and tangible cards that lift them up while they are in formation.

Overview

Goal: To affirm seminarians

Time of Year: Any, especially on special days like Christmas, Easter, Diaconate Ordination, Priestly Ordination, and/or birthday if that date is known.

Target Audience: Seminarians, Vocation Ministry members

Lead Time: 1 month

Implementation: Easy

People

External Leaders: None

VM Leaders: Ministry director, seminarian liaison or affirmation coordinator

Additional Volunteers: Ministry members to sign cards and help coordinate

Resources

Materials Needed: Cards to send to seminarians

Funds Needed: $30-50 for cards, depending on the number of seminarians

Number Expected: None

Promotion: N/A
Resources Available: None

Instructions

1. Consult the priest/pastor for input on implementation and for his blessing.
2. Determine who will coordinate the activity.
3. Decide on which special days cards will be given and how many seminarians will receive them. Consider asking the seminary staff for dates of ordinations and/or birthdays.
4. Send the cards at the appropriate times.

Notes:

—The ministry could take this idea one step further and buy $5-$10 gift cards to add to the card.
—This activity can be easily adapted for men and women in religious formation, as well.

ACTIVITY 52

Seminarian Welcome Back Gift

Consider giving the parish seminarians or all diocesan seminarians a small gift when they return to the seminary at the beginning of the fall semester. The gifts can be used to further their journey by helping them grow closer to Christ through inspirational books or other similar gifts.

Overview

Goal: To encourage local seminarians
Time of Year: Beginning of semester
Target Audience: Local seminarians, all of the Vocation Ministry members
Lead Time: 2 months
Implementation: Easy

People

External Leaders: None

VM Leaders: Director, seminarian liaison

Additional Volunteers: Ministry members to sign cards and help purchase gifts

Resources

Materials Needed: Greeting card; small gift (optional)

Funds Needed: Varies, depending on number of seminarians and gifts

Number Needed: One for each seminarian

Promotion: N/A

Resources Available: Find gift ideas at www.vocationministry.com

Instructions

1. Consult the priest/pastor for input on implementation and for his blessing.
2. Determine who will coordinate the activity.
3. Discuss possible gifts to present to seminarians and when to present them.
4. Obtain gifts and greeting cards for each seminarian.
5. Present welcome back packages.

Notes:

—One gift idea is *Mary and the Priestly Ministry*, which countless priests have found to be an inspiring book of meditation and a source of priestly renewal.

—This activity can be easily adapted for men and women in religious formation, as well.

PHASE IV

Ordination Reception

When a parishioner discerns and enters the seminary, a celebration is in order. When he is ordained to the priesthood, after years of prayer and study, the whole parish should rejoice. His ordination provides an opportunity for the local church community to affirm the young man's "Yes" to his vocation call, and the chance to celebrate together.

A newly-ordained priest's home parish typically has a Mass of Thanksgiving, which is one of his first celebrations of the Holy Mass as the presider. After that Mass, a reception provides time for parishioners to receive a First Blessing from the priest and fellowship. The event allows parishioners the opportunity to experience first-hand the joy of an ordination to the priesthood.

Overview

Goal: To affirm a newly ordained priest from the parish and inspire parishioners by his example

Time of Year: Normally in late May or June

Target Audience: Priest, parishioners

Lead Time: 6 months

Implementation: Complex

People

External Leaders: Priest to be ordained

VM Leaders: Priest, director, ordination coordinator, seminarian liaison, school liaison, affirmation coordinator, special events coordinator, communications coordinator, youth minister, Knights of Columbus liaison, faith formation liaison, ministries liaison, youth representative

Additional Volunteers: Ministry members to greet attendees; 2-12 adults and/or youth ministry for reception set-up and cleanup

Resources

Materials Needed: Gift for newly ordained priest, guest book, kneeler for first blessings (see Receptions on page 189)

Funds Needed: $300+, depending on food and decorations for reception, number attending, and donations

Number Expected: Varies, depending on the size of parish

Promotion: Publicize in bulletin, newsletter, website, and Mass announcements at least two months prior to event

Resources Available: Photos of ordination reception ideas at www.vocationministry.com.

Instructions

1. Consult the priest/pastor for input on implementation and for his blessing.
2. Determine who will coordinate the activity.
3. Discuss the event with the transitional deacon who is to be ordained to the priesthood, including which date he would like to have his Mass of Thanksgiving at the parish, making sure that to the extent possible his wishes for the reception are granted.
4. Determine a budget for the event, consulting with the pastor and/or parish administrator.
5. Coordinate a place for the reception with the parish facilities coordinator.
6. Communicate the date with all parish ministries. Mention this will be community-wide event and will only happen with everyone's support. Note that another email will be forthcoming with options on how to help. These include donating items or money, serving food or drink, and setting up before or cleaning up after the reception.
7. Ask the school principal, religious education director, and/or youth minister to have each student create a congratulations card or letter if the priest went to the parish school, or make one that all students sign if he did not.
8. Plan the reception, giving each participating group a task to oversee (see activity on page 189).
9. Provide all ministries and groups with suggestions of a gift for the priest to which all ministries may contribute, such as a porta-

ble Mass kit, Daily Roman Missal, Book of Blessings or Shorter Book of Blessings, vestment, chalice, or a gift certificate for a local Catholic bookstore. Cash is also a good option, as he may have a car or vestments to purchase. For a religious, who takes a vow of poverty, depending on his community, cash might not be the best gift. In some communities all cash gifts must be turned over to the prior of the house. The prior may allow a priest to keep the cash, only some of it, or none at all. In general, gift cards are a different matter and are not turned in.

10. Publicize through the bulletin, newsletter, website, and Mass announcements at least two months prior to the event.

11. Meet every few weeks or monthly to discuss arrangements.

12. Find out if the transitional deacon has family attending his reception so a table may be reserved for them. Also, a nice gesture is to give his family the flower arrangement or some token of appreciation for their sacrifices as parents of a new priest.

13. Set up for the event the day prior.

14. Request all ministry members to greet guests and make sure everything runs smoothly.

15. After the event, give the new priest his gifts.

16. Clean up afterward, which could be a task for one of the helping groups.

17. Write each parish ministry a note of appreciation for their contribution.

18. In the bulletin, thank all those who attended and helped, adding a picture or two to share this special event with the parish at large.

ACTIVITY 54

Remembrance of Deceased Priests And Religious

The Feast of All Souls, the day that the Church encourages the offering of prayers and Mass for the souls of the faithfully departed, is celebrated on November 2. In the early Church, the names of the men and women who passed away that year were posted in the church so that the community remembered them in prayer. Honoring the memory of the deceased priests and religious men and women, who either were from or served at the parish in some capacity, can be done in a number of ways. However the ministry decides to execute this activity, be assured the prayers that come from it will be fruitful.

Overview

Goal: To encourage prayer for the deceased priests and religious from the parish and/or those who served the parish in some official capacity

Time of Year: All Soul's Day (November 2)

Target Audience: Parishioners

Lead Time: 6 weeks

Implementation: Easy to moderate

People

External Leaders: Diocesan Archives and Records Department staff, if necessary

VM Leaders: Director, activities coordinator, communications coordinator

Additional Volunteers: None

Resources

Materials Needed: Varies, depending on activity selected

Funds Needed: $20 to print photos

Number Expected: Up to all parishioners

Promotion: Publicize through the bulletin one month prior, asking for anyone to send pictures and information about those deceased priest(s) or religious who attended the parish at one time; post photos of the deceased around parish

Resources Available: Photos of deceased may be available through Diocesan Archives and Records Department

Instructions

1. Consult the priest/pastor for input on implementation and for his blessing.
2. Determine who will coordinate the activity.

3. Ask the priest/pastor how the parish will celebrate the Feast of All Souls. If nothing is planned yet, suggest one of the following.

   - Place the names/pictures/dates of service/date of death of deceased priests and religious in the bulletin on the weekend before or after the Feast of All Souls
   - If available at the parish, place the names of deceased priests and religious in the parish "Book of Life" on the Feast of All Souls
   - If available at the parish, place the pictures and names of deceased priests and religious on display for the Feast of All Souls

4. If not readily available, request information and pictures of the priests who have served at the parish in some way from the Diocesan Archives and Records Department. The pictures can be placed in borrowed frames from ministry members. Send a thank-you note to each external leader, expressing the ministry's gratitude for their help in the success of the activity.

Notes:

—Consider including endearing stories about each priest/religious in the bulletin during each week of November.

ACTIVITY 55

Deacon Sunday

Deacons are fully ordained clergy, reporting directly to the bishop. Deacons deserve much affirmation from parishioners for their tireless work, proclaiming the word of God, giving homilies, performing baptisms, and witnessing marriages, among other responsibilities. The Vocation Ministry should consider celebrating its permanent deacons yearly to show them the gratitude of the parishioners.

Overview

Goal: To show appreciation for parish deacons

Time of Year: Any, could be around patron saint of deacons feast day: St. Stephen the Martyr (December 26), St. Lawrence of Rome (August 10), or St. Marinus (September 3)

Target Audience: Deacons, parishioners

Lead Time: 2-3 months

Implementation: Easy to complex

People

External Leaders: None

VM Leaders: Priest, director, affirmation coordinator, special events coordinator, communications coordinator

Additional Volunteers: 2-12 adults and/or youth ministry for reception set-up and cleanup

Resources

Materials Needed: See Receptions on page 189

Funds Needed: Varies, depending on scope and reception

Number Expected: Up to all deacons and entire parish

Promotion: Publicize through bulletin, newsletter, website, and Mass announcements at least one month prior to event

Resources Available: Deacon Logo can be downloaded and pictures at www.vocationministry.com

Instructions

1. Consult the priest/pastor for input on implementation and for his blessing.
2. Determine who will coordinate the activity.
3. Determine the date and scope of the event (prayer, reception, or both), coordinating with deacons to maximize attendance.
4. Plan the reception (see activity on page 189).
5. Plan Prayer Drive for deacon(s) (Optional) (see activity on page 59).
6. Invite deacons and their spouses at least two months in advance.
7. Publicize through bulletin, newsletter, website, and Mass announcements at least two months prior to the event.
8. Set up, enjoy, and clean up after the reception, if applicable.

9. In the bulletin, thank all those who attended, adding a picture or two to share this special event with the parish at large.

Notes:

—Consider holding two receptions, one in English and, if there are Masses said in a different language, consider a second reception after one of those Masses.

—Giving small flower arrangements to each deacon's spouse and family is a nice gesture of appreciation for their daily sacrifices.

ACTIVITY 56

Retired Priests and Religious Day

Priests and religious devote their lives in service to others, and when they retire, they should still feel the love of a parish community. A Vocation Ministry can help facilitate this in a simple way by organizing a prayer drive for them, or a card-writing campaign, or in a more complex manner with a full celebration. Whatever your ministry and parish is open to, take this opportunity to share love and appreciation with those who shared so much with all the Church.

Overview

Goal: To show appreciation for retired priests and religious
Time of Year: Any
Target Audience: Retired priests and religious, parishioners
Lead Time: 3 months
Implementation: Complex

People

External Leaders: Retirement community director or staff
VM Leaders: Priest, director, activity coordinator, affirmation coordinator, special events coordinator, communications coordinator
Additional Volunteers: 2-12 adults and/or youth ministry for reception set-up and cleanup

Resources

Materials Needed: See Receptions on page 189
Funds Needed: Varies, depending on reception and gift
Number Expected: Up to all retired priests and religious and parish
Promotion: Begin publicizing through bulletin, newsletter, website, and Mass announcements at least one month prior to event
Resources Available: N/A

Instructions

1. Consult the priest/pastor for input on implementation and for his blessing.
2. Determine who will coordinate the activity.
3. Determine the date of the event, collaborating with leader of retirement community if applicable.
4. Plan the reception (see activity on page 189), either at the retirement community or the parish. If at parish, coordinate with the parish facilities coordinator a place/date for the reception.
5. Decide if a small gift should be given to each retired priest or religious.
6. Invite retired priests and religious at least two months in advance.
7. Publicize through bulletin, newsletter, website, and Mass announcements at least two months prior to the event.
8. Provide transportation for retired priests and religious, if necessary.
9. Set up for, enjoy, and clean up after the reception.
10. In the bulletin, thank all those who attended, adding a picture or two to share this special event with the parish at large.
11. Send a thank-you note to each external leader, expressing the ministry's gratitude for their help in the success of the activity.

Notes:

—Consider asking parishioners to visit retired priests and religious on a regular basis, and to take goods or supplies to them as ongoing support.

Reception

Few activities can leave such an impression on the parish community as a well-planned reception. Bringing parishioners together—to honor clergy on their ordination anniversary, to say farewell to a religious sister who is moving, or for a myriad of other occasions—can be meaningful for all involved. Receptions affirm the clergy, married couples, or religious in such a special way, allowing parishioners the opportunity to give back and show their appreciation whether they help with the reception in some way, or just attend. Consider starting with a simple reception and then hosting larger, more complex receptions as your ministry grows in the parish.

Overview

Goal: To honor and affirm the guests of honor
Time of Year: Any
Target Audience: Parishioners; guest(s) of honor varies
Lead Time: 2-4 months
Implementation: Easy to complex

People

External Leaders: Consider who needs to be involved if guest of honor comes from outside of the parish or if reception is held off campus
VM Leaders: Priest, director, special event coordinator, communications coordinator
Additional Volunteers: Ministry members to help organize and staff event; 2-12 adults and/or youth ministry for set-up and cleanup
Resources Available: See pictures of various receptions at www.vocationministry.com

Simple Reception

A simple reception can be held at any time and during any phase. Normally they are held when few funds and/or volunteers are available, but that does not mean they are not impactful. A donut and coffee reception that has a few decorations and is well-publicized still means so much to the priests, religious, or whomever is receiving the affirmation. The main aspect of any reception is the parishioners showing up to express their appreciation and gratitude toward the recipient, so consider using a simple reception when your parochial vicar first arrives or a priest celebrates their 10th ordination anniversary.

Resources for Simple Reception

Supplies: Chairs, tables, serving supplies
Food: Appetizers such as cheese and crackers, vegetable trays, popcorn, cookies
Drink: Punch, tea, water
Decorations: Disposable tablecloths, greenery, personal Catholic artwork, pictures of the guest of honor
Funds Needed: < $50, depending on number attending, and how much is donated for the effort
Resources Available: See pictures of various receptions at www.vocationministry.com

Moderate Reception

A reception that contains more moving parts and requires at least 3-4 ministry members and more funding would be considered moderate. This reception could consist of finger foods such as sandwiches and chips and added options for drinks. More decorations, consisting of Catholic artwork, crosses, and/or statues can be used to spruce up the reception space. Consider placing pictures of the priest or guest of honor around the area, too, for a more personal touch. A moderate reception is perfect for saying farewell to a priest who has not been at the parish long, thanking the deacons for serving the church, or bringing parishioners together for fellowship before or after a vocation event.

Resources for Moderate Reception

Supplies: Chairs, tables, serving supplies, microphone(s), guest book, spiritual bouquet

Food: Appetizers such as cheese and crackers, vegetable trays, popcorn, cookies; heavy hors d'oeuvres, and desserts such as cake, cookies, and brownies

Drink: Punch, tea, water, soft drinks

Decorations: Disposable or linen tablecloths, greenery and/or flowers, personal Catholic artwork, pictures of the guest of honor

Funds Needed: < $200, depending on number attending, and how much is donated for the effort

Resources Available: See pictures of various receptions at www.vocationministry.com

---

Complex Reception

A complex reception is best undertaken by a more-experienced ministry that has plenty of funding and volunteers. This reception normally takes place after a special Mass for the priest or guest of honor and requires more substantial food, with either a buffet or sit down meal being served. Extensive decorations consist of artwork and flowers and pictures of the guest of honor. A printed program may be offered if speakers or activities are to take place during the reception. Consider showing a video tribute, especially if the guest of honor has been at the parish a long time. Another nice touch is to have a professional photographer present, preferably a parishioner, who can capture the special moments of the reception so that the guest of honor has a way of sharing the event with others. Then, have a ministry member make a memory book to give to the guest of honor as a final gift from the reception. This type of reception is perfect for when a pastor first arrives, leaves, or any priest or religious celebrates a significant anniversary of ordination or vows taken.

Resources for Complex Reception

Supplies: Chairs, tables, serving supplies, microphone(s), guest book, spiritual bouquet

Food: Full meal, possibly catered, with dessert

Drink: Punch, tea, water, soft drinks, alcohol (optional)

Decorations: Linen tablecloths, candles (fake or real), greenery and/or flowers, personal Catholic artwork, pictures of the guest of honor

Funds Needed: $500+, depending on number attending, and how much is donated for the effort

Instructions

1. With the guest of honor, determine the date, time, and location of the reception. Discuss favorite food options, as well.
2. Determine any guests, especially family members, who should be invited.
3. Invite the guests at least two months in advance, requesting an RSVP at least two weeks prior to the event.
4. Determine the program for the event.
5. Determine the food and drink. Considerations include the time of day of the Mass and reception, the target audience, and the budget. Remember that some food, drink, and supplies can be donated by Vocation Ministry members, other parish ministries, or parishioners at large. It also can be a potluck meal.
6. Determine the dishware (paper, plastic) serving supplies (disposable or nice), and napkins (paper or linen).
7. Determine the theme and decorations.
8. Determine the facility set-up and program needs, such as the arrangement of tables and chairs, podium, and microphone(s). Tables may be arranged in a circle, in a cross formation, or in cafeteria-style rows. Make sure the reception area is not too big for the number of expected attendees so there is an intimate feel to the room.
9. Donation baskets can be placed at the doors to help cover any costs or to give a large monetary gift to the guest of honor.
10. In the bulletin, thank all those who attended and helped, adding a picture or two to share this special event with the parish at large.
11. In the bulletin, thank all those who attended, adding a picture or two to share this special event with the parish at large.

CHAPTER EIGHT

PERSEVERANCE

"Persecutions are to the works of God what the frosts of winter are to plants. Far from destroying them, they allow them to strike their roots deeper in soil and make them more full of life." ~St. Alphonsus Liguori

When we go through a struggle, especially in His Holy Name, we grow. We are given an opportunity for God to open wider doors for His Kingdom's glory. Knowing this helps us to press on during difficult times. There is a purpose in each struggle. *His* purpose.

The success of a Vocation Ministry should be measured over years, not months, so leaders and participants are encouraged not to become frustrated with early roadblocks or with what feels like slow progress. The mission of creating a more vocation-minded parish will not be accomplished overnight, but the ministry is reaching its goal with every prayer drive, festival booth, or speaker at the parish.

When the ministry faces adversity or resistance, especially within the church community, it is easy to become discouraged. However, if the volunteers keep a positive attitude and continue with meaningful, uplifting activities, eventually they will win over even the most skeptical of critics. Perseverance and prayer will be the ministry's most valuable virtues throughout this vocation adventure.

Some years, the workers will be plenty and the fields will be ripe for harvest, with strong interest in vocations. Other years, a parish may find it difficult to recruit a Vocation Ministry leader or more members, and the ministry may diminish for a period of time. Keep in mind that progress and transformation happen in God's time.

Personal Ministry Highlight

When Father Victor Perez was transferred to another parish after two amazing years at Saint Cecilia, our ministry had to do some serious soul searching. Our members wondered what we would do without Father Victor leading us. Though those same thoughts and fears crossed my mind, I felt quite certain that God would not have sent us this holy priest to inspire us and pave the way for our events only for us to falter and crumble when he left. Our ministry needed to carry on this work, relying even more on the Holy Spirit to guide us. He taught us how to fish, so we needed to keep casting our nets each and every day.

I cannot tell you that this has been easy, but I am convinced that one of the purposes in all of the change and struggle is for us to relate more fully to others who persevere in vocation work without such full support and guidance from their priest. Though our work continues, we are told "no" much more often. More barriers are placed in our way. We cling to Jesus more fully and persist, knowing that this is God's ministry, and that we're striving to do His will.

One of Saint Junípero Serra's first homilies sums up how a ministry can view suffering: "Serra tells the story of a hermit who had a long way to walk to get his water. He considered moving his hermitage closer to the spring. One day while he was going back, burdened with his jug, he heard a voice calling, 'One, two, three, four.' He stopped, looked around, saw nobody, and kept walking. But the voice continued counting … 'five, six, seven, eight,' and said, 'I am an angel sent by God to count the steps you take so that none is left without reward.' The hermit moved his hermitage, indeed, further from the fountain!"[18]

Instead of complaining to others or feeling abandoned, a ministry grows stronger by embracing those times when the work is most difficult and can carry on knowing that none is left without reward.

Finally, encourage one another, encourage the priest or pastor who supports the ministry, celebrate victories large and small, cul-

---

18 Orfalea, Gregory. Journey to the Sun: Junípero Serra's Dream and the Founding of California. N.p.: n.p., n.d. Electronic.

tivate peace and collaboration among the ministry members and the volunteers, and pray, pray, pray without ceasing.

AFTERWORD

In Pope Francis' first homily as pope, he said that the Church is not an NGO (non-governmental organization) which is self-absorbed. We are the Church, the bride of Christ. We bear witness to Christ, that He is alive. He is risen! You who are beginning this Vocation Ministry must realize this. Jesus is alive. He is not just a memory, a teacher who left us a path to follow. He is the Lord in our midst who actively calls people to follow Him in His vineyard right now.

It is He who works within and without us through His Spirit. He is calling priests and sisters to be his channels of grace and to bear him witness. He called the apostles, the first men with whom he shared his priesthood and sent them out to teach in his name baptizing in the name of the Father, Son, and Holy Spirit. Today he needs his brother priests to continue this ministry and do what he commanded at the Last Supper so that He can continually appear in the "breaking of the bread" (Luke 24:35). He calls them to go and forgive sins in His name as he told them shortly after he rose from the dead (John 20:23).

I venture to say that there is nothing dearer to His heart than this ministry of being a "fisher of men" in the service of vocations. What a beautiful and selfless way to participate in Jesus' mission by helping him to find his coworkers. We fish for all types of people for the kingdom. All are called to follow Jesus. But, what if we catch a future fisherman? A priest, sister or brother? This ministry of vocations will help all people to be more attentive to Jesus' call to follow him in whatever vocation he calls them in for the good of His kingdom. It is not popular to follow Him. It is not the way of the world, but it is truly an adventure.

I encourage those of you in Vocation Ministry to surrender to God's call. Don't be afraid of it, even in your day-to-day lives. The Spirit will do awesome things through you.

And let us follow Jesus' advice: Pray! "Pray earnestly to the Lord of the harvest to send out laborers into his harvest" (Matthew 9:35). At Saint Cecilia Catholic Church we recruited the best prayer warrior around: Mary! We placed our whole ministry in Mary's hands. She is the first disciple of Jesus from her "Yes" at the Annunciation to her acceptance of God's will at the foot of the cross when she was given the role of being our Mother (cf. John 19:26,27). We need her emptiness, her poverty of spirit, her attentiveness to the Word of God. With her prayers and example you can create a culture of listening to His call in your parish beginning with your ministry.

Come Holy Spirit. Fill the Hearts of your Faithful. Enkindle in them the fire of your love. Send forth your Spirit and renew the face of the earth.

Father Victor Perez

SAMPLE ANNUAL BUDGETS

Below are some sample budgets from a Vocation Ministry. Notice that the budgets are categorized by each area of ministry: Prayer, Awareness and Education, Youth, and Affirmation. This arrangement makes it easier for the parish financial committee to read and support the ministry's endeavors as they are well-rounded.

Sample Annual Budget, Phase I—Small Parish

PRAYERS

Spiritual bouquets	$50
Priesthood Sunday	
Bulletin announcement and intercessory prayers	
Prayer Drive for Priests signage	$20
World Day of Prayer for Vocations	
Prayer cards	$150

AWARENESS and EDUCATION

Book rack materials	
World Day for Consecrated Life	
Informational flier about consecrated life	$20
Festival booth	
Booth rental fee	$50
Giveaways (candy)	$50

YOUTH

National Vocations Awareness Week

Vocation pamphlets for teens in confirmation prep	$30
Reception for guests visiting classrooms	$40
Stipend to speakers and religious guests	$100

AFFIRMATION

Donut Reception for Ordination Anniversary

Food	$100
Decorations	$40

Gifts

Priests on their special days	$100
TOTAL EXPENSES	**$750**

Sample Annual Budget, Phase II—Large Parish

PRAYER

Spiritual bouquets

Printing	$50

Priesthood Sunday

Prayer cards	$150
Prayer drive for priests signage	$100

World Day of Prayer for Vocations

Rosary rings	$150
Fliers	$50
Daily Mass prayer cards, English and Spanish	$200

AWARENESS and EDUCATION

Book rack materials	$50

World Day for Consecrated Life

Fliers/posters	$100

Discerner support (Books for priests to hand out)

To Save a Thousand Souls	$80

Festival booth

    Booth rental fee $125

    Giveaways (Frisbees, bumper stickers, candy, etc.) $250

YOUTH

National Vocations Awareness Week

    Promotional materials Life Teen $120

    Reception for guests visiting classrooms $60

    Stipend for religious guests $200

    Prayer cards for children and adults $180

Altar server appreciation

    BBQ dinner $250

    Decorations $40

    Stipend to speakers and religious guests $50

AFFIRMATION

Reception for Anniversary of Ordination

    Food $500

    Decorations $40

Gifts

    Priests on their special days $200

TOTAL EXPENSES   **$2,945**

SAMPLE YEARLY CALENDAR

Ministry Highlights 2014-15

August

4th	Adoration for Vocations
19th	Meeting

September

2nd	Adoration for Vocations
14th	9 a.m. Instillation Mass/Reception for new pastor
16th	Meeting 6:30-8 p.m.

October

4th	Fr. Frank's birthday
5th	Parish festival booth
7th	Adoration for Vocations
21st	Meeting 6:30-8 p.m.
26th	Priesthood Sunday

November

1st	All Soul's Day-Pray for our deceased priests
2nd	National Vocation Awareness Week-Mass kickoff
4th	Adoration for Vocations
5th	Classrooms visits at parish school
7th	Junior High Vocation night
18th	Meeting 6:30-8 p.m.

December

2nd	Adoration for Vocations
8th	Fr. Gabriel's Ordination Anniversary
16th	Meeting 6:30-8 p.m.

January

6th	Adoration for Vocations
11th	Vocation Panel at Confirmation Prep assembly
20th	Meeting 6:30-8 p.m.

February

3rd	Adoration for Vocations
8th	World Day for Consecrated Life-Posters
17th	Meeting 6:30-8 p.m.
21st	Altar Server Celebration
27th	Knights of Columbus Fish Fry for Vocations

March

4th	Adoration for Vocations
17th	Meeting 6:30-8 p.m.
22nd	Fr. Frank's Ordination Anniversary

April

5th	Adoration for Vocations
14th	Meeting 6:30-8 p.m.
26th	World Day of Prayer for Vocations

May

15th	Fr. Gabriel's birthday
17th	Transitional Diaconate Ordination
19th	Ministry End-of-Year Celebration 6:30-8 p.m.

June

6th	Diocesan Priesthood Ordinations- 10 a.m.

VOCATION DEFINITIONS

W hether beginning a new Vocation Ministry or enhancing or re-energizing an existing one, it helps if you and your ministry members have a rich understanding of vocations. This includes gaining knowledge about the discernment process that priests and religious go through, and the process of priestly ordination, as well as the equally important vocation of marriage.

Apostolic—A word to describe religious orders that are more active in society and the world, perhaps performing services such as teaching, ministering to the sick, or going on mission to proclaim the Gospel.

Charism—The distinctive spirituality of the founder or foundress of a religious institute. It is the "personality" of a religious community bequeathed by the one who founded it.

Convent—A residential community for religious sisters.

Cloister—Residence or living area for secluded nuns who rarely leave their community.

Contemplative—A word used to describe a religious order that holds prayer as its principal activity.

Diocesan priest—A priest is ordained to preach the Gospel and celebrate the sacraments. When a man receives the sacrament of Holy Orders at ordination, he makes three promises: to pray the Liturgy of the Hours daily, to obey his bishop, and to live a celibate life. Diocesan priests serve the people of a particular geographic region.

Discernment—The process of prayerfully discovering over a period of time whether or not a person is called to a particular vocation.

Evangelical counsels—The advice given by Jesus to certain individuals regarding voluntary poverty, chastity, obedience.

Final Vows—Formal commitments made by a religious man or woman to God to follow Jesus in his poverty, chastity, and obedience.

Holy Orders—The sacrament by which men become deacons, priests and bishops. The mission entrusted by Christ to his apostles continues to be exercised in the church through prayer and the laying on of hands. By receiving holy orders men's souls are marked with a permanent, sacramental character.

Novice—The second formal stage of becoming a consecrated religious when a man or woman a studies to learn more about the religious community, his or her relationship with God, and the lifetime commitment to the religious life. This stage may take one to two years of prayer.

Postulant—The first formal stage of becoming a consecrated religious that normally takes 6-12 months to complete.

Religious life—Men and women who make public vows of poverty, chastity, and obedience, and who live this permanent state of life in a community recognized by the Church. This includes sisters, nuns, brothers, and monks. Some religious men are also ordained priests.

Seminary—A place where a young man goes to prepare for the priesthood. Seminaries have four areas of formation: spiritual, intellectual, human, and pastoral. A man would typically attend seminary for eight years after high school. If he goes to seminary after college, the length of study is typically six years.

Vocation—A calling or summoning. A vocation is God's invitation to love and serve him and his Church in a particular way of life. It is a call to live on earth in a way that will impact eternity. The word itself is derived from the Latin word *vocare*.